What to Know Before They Go:
College Edition

What to Know Before They Go: College Edition

Pamela Ellis, MBA, PhD

The Education Doctor®

Copyright

Five Smooth Stones Publishing
3490 S. Dixie Dr. Suite 225
Dayton, OH 45439
theeducationdoctor.com
(855) 447-2388

Printed in USA

ISBN-13: 978-1976409325
ISBN-10: 1976409322

Ordering Information:
Quantity sales and special discounts are available on volume purchases by schools, associations, and others. For details, contact the "Special Sales Department" at the address above.

Disclaimer

The information in this book is believed to be accurate. The author is not responsible for any errors or omissions or changes made in any of the website links or references made in this book, or for the results obtained from the use of this information, or future changes now made in existing material (i.e., college forms, or other). The author has made every effort to ensure that the information in this book is correct at press time, and she hereby disclaims any liability to any party for any loss, damage, or disruption caused by any errors, omissions, or changes, regardless of the cause of such. All information in this book is provided on an "as is basis," with no guarantee of the results obtained from the use of this information.

Dedication

To Robert, Jan, Miles and Vera Grace

for all of who you are and who I am because of you

Contents

Acknowledgements

There's a scripture that begins, "If it had not been for the Lord ..." and it reminds me of where my strength and energy comes from ... Thank you Lord for the vision and calling you have placed on my life.

An endeavor such as this can't be done alone. So many people, places and events have made this book possible. It's very likely that I will miss a name or two. If so, please count it to my head and not my heart. I'm very grateful to each of you and your support.

Robert. For all your loving support of my entrepreneurial endeavors and being the best partner in parenting. We have always been a unified voice on educating and raising our children.

Jan, Miles and Vera Grace. I would not have been able to add the rich insight without each of you being who you are as individuals. Your honesty, patience and unconditional love kept me encouraged through this project. Jan, you are my first born, first student and first book editor ... wow! Special shout outs to "Mama" and "Papa" Menafee and The Blue Family.

Siblings–Lou (Art), James (Mable), Dorothy, Tracy (Robert), Ann, Karen, Ronnie and Gwen (Larry)–and nieces and nephews–especially Tarus Richardson–for continuing to be there, attending my events, listening to my vents, and providing wisdom at the right time. My special Aunt Sweet, Kurt "KC" and Tricie Clayton.

A tremendous community of friends and colleagues who have encouraged and mentored me over the years: Rachel

Anderson, Darnel Barnes, Melissa Baten-Caswell, Delise Bernard, Carol Bernstein, Debbie Bradley, Donielle Buie, Dante Connell, Anthony Daniel, Autumn Drayton, Rachel Elahee, Pam Fay, Cheryl Gray, Toni Hall Parker, Diane Hirakawa, April House, Ellen Ireland, Naila Iscandari, Janet Jackson, Mia Jackson, Terrence Johnson, Damon Jones, James Jordan, Chris Judge, Nikki and Arnett Klugh, Meghan and George Knight, Tom Lasley, David Lawrence, Marie Leggon Wrighten, Abigail Levy, Kym Lew Nelson, Kathy Lofton, Kimberly Lovings, Brett Mahoney, Charlotte McGuire, Carolyn Misick, Fentriss Moore, Kathryn Mullen-Upton, Stephanie Newman, Natalie and Charles Okeke, Mark Parks, Valeria Perry, Melissa Persons, Christine Rafal, Urmee Siraj, Joyce Stone, Ty Stone, Susan Strong, Sadie Temple, Tanya Taul, Michelle Terry, Karen Townsend, Bevanne and Jeff Upperman, Barbara Wallace, Regina Wallace-Jones, Pamela and Desmoine West, Kevin Whitmore, Elizabeth Williams, Yvonne Young-Jones, and Cassandra Youngblood.

Client families. I have learned so much from our conversations and the thoughtful questions you raise. You keep me on my feet and challenge me to keep growing and serving to my best potential. Special shout outs to The Cole Family, Danis Family, Gupta Family, Hunt Family, Hyman Family, Kleiner Family, Mayeux Family, Ritter Family, Shephard Family, Washington Family, and Williams Family.

Parent groups and staff of Bellbrook High, Centerville City Schools, Deerfield Academy, Jack and Jill of America, Oakwood City School District, and The Miami Valley School for your continuous support of my work and nurturing my children. Special thanks to Wilberforce University for embracing me into your community, Pastor Washington and Phillips Temple for covering me in prayer since my Ohio arrival and Stanford National Black Alumni Association for being a strong supporter since Day 1.

Magnus Glen Christon (1967-2017)–a dear friend ... I'm eternally grateful for your unwavering support through the years.

Introduction:
An Ode to Parents Everywhere

This book is for parents who want their children to go to college and reach their full potential in life. As one of those parents, I have dedicated my life to establishing a solid foundation for my children and navigating each stage of their schooling. As a business owner, I have also successfully coached and guided the educational journey of countless other children. Ninety-five percent of my students have been admitted to their top-choice colleges and received up to $300,000 in scholarships per college, with an average of $75,000. I will tell you how I've achieved these stellar results and how you can help your teen get into his/her best-fit college and earn scholarships.

This book is my story of excelling beyond my parents' ability to support my education and helping kids everywhere to do the same. Most parents dream that their kids will do better than they did, particularly through higher education, but don't always have the resources or time to do so. That's where I was when growing up.

My parents did not know how to guide me through the education system because they had not gone through it themselves. My mother, Vera, left school after 8th grade to sharecrop, while my father, Henry, dropped out in 10th grade so that he could start working for a living. They both continued to maintain steady jobs and support our family of nine children, but couldn't help any of us pursue higher education. I realized early on that any accomplishment I earned educationally would be without the help of my parents. I was fortunate as I was placed into the Memphis City Schools' new accelerated program in 4th grade which helped me develop critical thinking skills and introduced me to a community of other high-achieving students.

Still, I learned from my parents' examples. Along with their steady day jobs, both maintained small businesses. These "side hustles" were never formalized, but they earned modest extra money through selling their skills. My mother was well-known as the best seamstress around, tailoring and making men's suits. My father sold snacks and drinks from his trunk in the factory's parking lot and mowed lawns in wealthy neighborhoods on the weekends. Seeing their perseverance and innovation profoundly influenced my belief in the importance of being resourceful.

Being the youngest of nine children, I also learned to receive the advice of others. My siblings were much older and already had their own families by the time I reached my teenage years. Only my oldest sister Lou, who lived in California, had attended a four-year institution at the time. Long distance phone calls were very expensive back then so when it came time to apply to college, I spent hours in the library reading books about college admissions and talking with teachers and classmates about college.

When I took standardized tests during high school, it opened new educational avenues for me because colleges and programs could get my contact information and mail me their own reading materials. One such program that mailed me an invitation to apply was the LEAD (Leadership Education and Development) Program in Business. Completing that application in the 11th grade gave me a taste for what college applications would be like, as I had to submit transcripts, test scores, teacher recommendations, and writing samples. Taking that leap of faith to apply and then attend this summer program emboldened me to keep applying myself to other competitive programs.

I applied to sixteen colleges... by hand. For the few applications that could be typed, I used a typewriter to tediously strike the letter keys onto the squared forms. My college list was a mix of colleges which included local colleges I had heard about, those who mailed me brochures (i.e., Stanford), and those listed in the guidebook rankings (i.e., any Ivy League).

On April 15, 1984, I asked one of my classmates to drive me home during the school lunch break so that I could check the mail. When I got several thick envelopes with acceptance and financial award letters, it was a dream come true, yet a tough decision for my family. My mother did not want me to leave Tennessee and had never heard of these far away colleges. The farthest one was a place called Stanford University. Most people in my hometown of Memphis, Tennessee, at that time, thought that Stanford was located in Connecticut and so did I until I saw the return address. After many frustrating conversations and intense convincing, my mother supported my decision to go there. Can you believe my mother and I rode a Greyhound bus from Tennessee to California?

Now, over thirty years later, my own children have attended out-of-state summer programs since 4th grade, have gone to boarding prep school in New England, and now attend Georgetown and Stanford. It's been emotionally hard to let my children go away from home even though I do this work. But just as my mother "let me go," I owe it to my children to let them reach their fullest potential.

Because I work with schools, community-based organizations, and families, I have the privilege of discussing education with parents from all walks of life, some with graduate degrees and those, like my own parents, with little or any formal education. But, a common thread among all these parents is that they want what is best for their children. You, the reader, are one of those parents (biologically, adoptive, or embraced).

The purpose of this book is to take the journey with you and guide you through what you need to know to help your teen reach his or her best potential. I wrote this book expressly for those who want to be intentional about their child's education, regardless of his/her income, background, or educational attainment.

In my work, I have personally coached and guided hundreds of parents and teens through the college admissions process. Those teens have attended summer programs around the world that I recommended and have been admitted to their top choice colleges like Amherst, Colorado College, Columbia, Harvard, Johns Hopkins, Morehouse, Oberlin, Santa Clara, The Ohio State University, Tuskegee, VCU, William and Mary, and Yale. (See theeducationdoctor.com/whattoknow for full list of colleges). But, these acceptances came after a lot of time and effort on all fronts and yours truly, The Education Doctor®.

Parents can do this work of learning about the college admissions process sooner or later. My hope is that regardless of where you are in taking this journey, this book will give you that additional insight and encouragement that can only come from my gifts, talent, and wisdom. So before I start "pouring" into you, I will tell you my overall beliefs about going to college, which I refer to as A+ Attitudes™.

- It's all about fit!
- There's a lot of money out there.
- Distance doesn't matter.

My beliefs are grounded in years of research and experience working with teens and parents. It will be one thing for you to read this book and know the steps in the college admissions process. However, my hope for you is that the numerous tips and bonus pullouts in this book will encourage you to move beyond knowing to DO what it takes for your teen to achieve their educational goals!

Part I
Building a Foundation
for Achievement

Chapter 1
Get Your Mindset Right

Every day, I partner with parents and teens to help them achieve their educational goals. As much as I love what I do, it's hard for me to avoid these conversations in my day-to-day life outside of the office. Once parents find out about my business, they only want to talk about their kids' education and ask for advice on what they should do. I listen, and almost always, they start on a path of explaining what they've done and justifying their actions with common myths like:

- My family won't qualify for any scholarships.
- Going to a state university will be better and cheaper than any private school.
- My kid's gotta be well-rounded to get into college.

Although these beliefs have permeated American culture for the past thirty years, I find them misguided because they shortchange the teen's options for reaching his/her best potential.

These parents mean well and believe in the importance of higher education for their children to be successful in life, but those same parents are also often too busy to take on the college admissions process by themselves. Add the overwhelming concerns over rising tuition and competition to get in, and now more than ever, the intimidation of applying to schools causes many to procrastinate. Too many parents and teens are waiting until senior year to start the college admissions process, which leads to fewer college options and scholarships.

It is exactly because the college admissions process is very expensive and very competitive that I know parents should start even earlier than junior year to start looking for college options and scholarships which brings us to my one precondition.

This Process Takes More Time and Effort Than You Think

It takes parents over 300 hours to help their teen through the college admissions process. Most parents don't have that kind of time to spare. And unfortunately, most parents don't realize that this much of their time is necessary until too late in the process. It's worse too when parents use this time for worry rather than productively taking actions to support their teen.

The parents who take on the challenge of being their teen's college counselor usually spend more time than otherwise would be necessary because there is a learning curve which is steep and time consuming. Learning this role thoroughly enough to help your own teen requires extensive research and reliable resources.

I've spent over twenty years researching and visiting college campuses which helps me match schools to the particular students I work with. Also, my firm has its own online college database that makes it easier for me to gather information more efficiently. I save parents over 150 hours of their time by vetting colleges and putting in the one-on-one time with their teen. I wrote this book to help significantly reduce parents' learning curve.

With this understanding of the true time commitment, my three A+ Attitudes™ establish the mindset you must have in order to be successful in the college admissions process.

Bear with me as my advice directly counters many of the commonly held beliefs parents have about where and how their teens go to college. Follow these guidelines and I promise that you will be satisfied with the results.

A+ Attitudes™ #1 - It's All About Fit

We all fall victim to judging colleges based on their name, reputation, price tag, location, rumors, personal opinions, and most other qualities except for the most important one: FIT–how compatible will a college be with your teen's specific academic interests, social needs, vocational interests, and your family's financial situation. Ultimately, "fit" is what gives your teen the best chance of thriving and finishing. All the other attributes have little to no influence on whether a teen stays in college from freshman to sophomore year or eventually graduates. An important book that informed my thinking on this is *Crossing the Finish Line: Completing College at America's Public Universities* which highlights the fact that over half of college students do not graduate. A profound finding from the book is that the breakdown actually happens in the application process. When teens apply and go to colleges that are not a good fit for them, they are more likely to drop out! And... just because a college has a brand name doesn't mean that it's an automatic fit for your teen.

When I work with students privately on developing their college list, writing compelling essays, and even negotiating their offers, my focus is on how well the student and the college "fit." The notion of "fit" is the primary driver for admissions and scholarships. There are four areas of fit that I reference when I work with students privately: Academic, Social, Vocational, and Financial. (Although I refer to college fit here, this term is also relevant to high schools, which I will discuss in the next chapter, "Prepare Before High School.")

Academic Fit

"Academic Fit" refers to how the faculty teaches, the academic priorities of the college, and what the learning environment is like. When it comes to academic fit, there are distinct curriculum offerings that a college may offer. A college may offer an open curriculum, a core curriculum, or a distributed curriculum. Open curriculum means that students are free to choose which classes they want to take. Several colleges with an open curriculum include Brown University and Amherst College. A core curriculum means that there are specific courses that all students must take regardless of their majors, and the most well-known institution with a core curriculum is Columbia University in New York. The majority of US colleges have a distributed curriculum which is a hybrid of a core and open curriculum. For example, a college with a distributed curriculum may require that students take a natural sciences course. However, within that category of natural sciences, there could be any number of courses from which students can choose. These academic distinctions matter to your teen's success throughout college. So in the application process, you should be sure that your teen's college options are a match to the college's teaching style and level of rigor so your teen will thrive academically during college.

Social Fit

"Social Fit" refers to whether the social environment matches with your teen's interests and needs. Perhaps a large university with athletics, lots of clubs, and extensive social activities matches with your teen's maturity and responsibility. Or would your teen feel more comfortable in a smaller setting, coed, or single-gender? In the freshman year in particular, the social adjustment is key for transitioning well to college life. The social fit really speaks to the culture of the campus and the potential for your own teen to thrive within that environment. To really get to know a campus socially, students must visit it in person. The internet is no substitute for sitting in the dining hall, talking with students about their clubs, or walking on campus at night to see if you feel safe.

Another important aspect of the social adjustment to college is whether or not to have a roommate. I applaud the colleges that still spend time with matching freshmen roommates. In too many instances, I have seen students shortchange their freshman year experience by foregoing the university's roommate selection system and choosing their own roommate, mainly through social media. Even if the matched roommate isn't the best choice in the end, it teaches students how to deal with unfamiliar situations... a part of growing up.

Vocational Fit

"Vocational Fit" matters whether or not a teen knows his/her career interests. Let's say, for example, that your teen is interested in veterinary medicine. There are certain colleges that support that area of interest with pre-professional clubs, faculty involved in research, or a track record of admission to graduate programs. Those colleges that match with that career interest should then be researched and visited to perhaps apply for admission. If your teen, on the other hand, is "undecided", then there are also colleges that can support his/her changing interests. The college's career placement office may also have programs to guide teens through internships, shadow opportunities, or community service that prepare for careers after college.

Financial Fit

The "Financial Fit" refers to the types and availability of merit and financial aid opportunities for your family to make college affordable. Financial fit has nothing to with sticker

13

price but has everything to do with reading the fine print and meeting with appropriate university officials to negotiate the best offer. Fine print details include researching these key statistics:

- Cost of attendance (tuition, fees, books, travel, miscellaneous expenses)
- Percent of financial need met
- Percent of students that receive financial support
- Special funding programs

Even if a family thinks that they won't qualify for any financial support, they should still apply, i.e., complete the FAFSA (Free Application for Federal Student Aid) and/or CSS (College Scholarship Service) Profile for two reasons. The first reason to submit any financial forms is to be considered for "need-based" scholarships. You must remember though... how you define "need" may not be the same as how the college defines your "need." One of my students received an additional $12,000 in scholarships just because his parents completed FAFSA. His parents were pleasantly surprised and felt that the thirty minutes spent to complete the FAFSA was worth it. The second reason to submit any financial forms is to be eligible for future financial awards during college. For many colleges, if a family doesn't apply before the freshman year, then they may not be able to apply later during college. So, to keep the option available in case of any unforeseen event while your teen is in college, parents should apply prior to freshman year.

I will discuss financial fit more as I elaborate on the next A+ Attitudes™.

A+ Attitudes™ #2 - There's a Lot of Money Out There

At every level of the education system, there's money available to make it more affordable than it would be otherwise. As a beneficiary of scholarships for my own children to attend private schools from middle school through college, I know this for a fact personally. Likewise, when I have worked with students attending private K-12 schools, they also have been awarded scholarships. The scholarships are typically provided by the schools.

There are, however, numerous outside scholarships available to pay for private K-12 schooling. A Better Chance, Inc. and Caroline Bradley are two of the more popular scholarship providers. In order to obtain these scholarships though, families must plan ahead. For example, when my own children applied to Caroline Bradley, I reviewed the entire application about two years ahead of their application date so that I would be familiar with the criteria for them to submit a competitive application.

In the same way, scholarships for college require some planning ahead in order for students to have a chance to earn those awards. For example, many scholarships require a writing sample. The writing sample can be a graded assignment or an essay in response to a basic prompt. Therefore, your teen at the least must be comfortable with writing. Usually, the more lucrative the scholarship, the more writing will be required. The advance planning is critical for these scholarships because good writing skills are developed over time. The Caroline Bradley Scholarship, for example again, requires essays. Because my sons attended elementary schools with strong writing expectations and had written essays for summer programs, they were well-prepared to write the lengthy essays required for their Caroline Bradley Scholarship submission in seventh grade.

The other way that parents can plan ahead is by applying earlier. There are scholarships that teens can apply to as early as age 13. Too many families start searching for scholarships in their teen's senior year of high school. If the senior year is the first time that a family starts searching for scholarships, their chances of obtaining any outside scholarships will be diminished.

A very popular scholarship that students can only apply to in 12th grade is the Coca-Cola Scholarship. It's a prestigious, well-funded scholarship. The initial selection criteria are based on transcripts, i.e. GPA, and test scores from about 6,000+ applicants. Having a strong GPA and high test scores takes time and effort. But once students pass this first round and are considered for the next stage, they must submit numerous writing assignments and interview. This review process whittles down to only 150 awards. (To put this in perspective, that would be a less than a two percent acceptance rate!)

However, the larger awards, and with better odds, come directly from the colleges. Just as colleges recruit athletes by offering scholarships for them to play a sport, colleges also recruit students for all sorts of reasons. The term used to refer to these different types of recruiting efforts is "merit scholarships." The "merit" part of the scholarship is defined by each college based on its institutional priorities. A tip for learning the institutional priorities is to read the college president's letter, often available online. If the college president mentions that a new science lab is being built, then there's a strong chance that "merit scholarships" will be offered to science applicants. If a college, for example, has a priority to maintain the strength of its marching band, then aspiring applicants who have the talent to participate in the marching band will likely be awarded a "merit scholarship" as an enticement to accept the admissions offer. (I use the term "admissions offer" because it is negotiable.)

So, I can't stress enough the mistake of judging a college by its sticker price. Eighty percent of the families who have children attending college are getting some money for college. A key data point that you can review for the colleges is the percentage of their students that receive scholarships.

Families I work with every year are surprised by the merit scholarships their teens receive. It's especially surprising to those who make a financial investment to work with my firm to save their time, yet get a financial return when their teen is offered a merit scholarship (without even having to disclose their tax returns).

Another aspect to the financial support is the gap between scholarships from private versus public universities. When my students want to apply only to public colleges because of the sticker price, I encourage them to also consider a few comparable private colleges on their list. A recent trend I've noticed is that private colleges tend to have higher merit awards than the public universities. For my own children and several of my students, the private colleges offered more scholarships than the flagship public university in their home state. Thus, it was less expensive to pay tuition and fees to a private college out-of-state rather than pay in-state tuition and fees.

As I said at the outset, there's more money for college than you think.

A+ Attitudes™ #3 - Distance Doesn't Matter

When my two sons left for boarding school at ages 15 and 16, I had a difficult time with them being so far away from home. Even though our family made the decision together, releasing the sense of control over their lives posed the greatest challenge to my enthusiasm for their new school 800 miles away. I could no longer be there for every sports-related injury or problem with friends and teachers, let alone homesickness. With these risks in mind too, parents in our community could not imagine why we would make such a decision at all, and especially before college. But we made this choice because we believed a boarding prep school environment would afford opportunities far beyond what a local school could offer our sons. Most importantly, my sons *wanted* to go. As much as I worried about how far away they would be, I knew that making them stay home would emotionally drive them away from me which could do much more harm than their being physically away at boarding school.

This perspective is part of why I get frustrated when I hear parents say that they want their teen to be close to home. I understand the codependency between parents and children and/or the financial concerns of travel, but limiting your teen's college list to local schools ultimately limits their opportunities to thrive during college. Research shows that students who go further away from home for college–especially girls–actually experience a greater sense of academic confidence, leadership skills, and emotional *well-being*. Aware of these benefits, many colleges, in turn, prioritize geographic diversity in admissions. Those colleges would like to see students from as many different states and countries on their campuses as possible and oftentimes offer scholarships to distant applicants because of the geographic diversity and benefits those students would contribute to campus life.

Nevertheless, the most important person in this process is your teen, the college-bound student. The key to mastering this particular A+ Attitudes™ is having the conversation about distance earlier in the college admissions process and telling yourself and your teen that distance doesn't matter. If your teen wants to apply to schools close to home, great! If he/she wants to apply to schools far from home, also great! Ask your teen if he/she likes how the different schools "fit" to ensure that his/her wanting to apply to these schools is for good reasons, and if the answers are for good reasons, then support your teen's decision wholeheartedly.

Chapter 2
Prepare Before High School

Middle school is a transformative time for our children. Although most middle schools in the US may start at 5th or 6th grade, the middle school years really start in 4th grade. A significant change for 4th grade is the emphasis on reading comprehension. A common way to refer to this curriculum change is that up to 3rd grade, students are learning to read, but 4th grade is reading to learn. This academic change through middle school is significant but then is compounded with all the developmental changes that come from puberty which is happening at the same time.

For me personally, I felt that pre-4th grade was the time that I really became even more intentional about my children's education, especially my sons. There are a number of reports and studies about the declining interest in school for Black males around 4th grade. To confront the risk of them losing interest in school, I actively found ways to help out in their classroom and got very creative when it came to making learning fun and keeping them engaged during the summer breaks.

I was very mindful too of their friends and their friends' parents. I didn't want my sons growing up too soon like I had. When I was in 7th grade, my mother allowed me to spend the night with a girlfriend from school. I witnessed things at that friend's home that were well beyond my pre-teen ability to comprehend. If my mother had known more about my girlfriend's parents, I don't think she would have allowed me to spend the night.

Whenever my children had "play dates" with school-mates, I always asked them about their time away and how the friend's parents treated them. One time, when I asked my younger son about a playdate at a friend's home, he told me that the parents had handcuffed their son to the staircase. Something about hearing that made me very uneasy, and I didn't allow him to have play dates at that family's home again.

Form Good Habits Sooner Rather than Later

Grades and extracurricular activities don't officially count yet for college, but middle school is where you and your teen can lay a strong foundation for their success throughout high school. The strength of that foundation will be tested again and again throughout high school, especially when your teens may want to exert their own independence and defy your rules. Establishing a firm foundation and values while in middle school can help mitigate these trials that are naturally part of adolescence.

Keep Reading

Reading is key to a successful transition from middle school to high school. It's easier said than done to encourage your teen to read. One of the biggest mistakes that parents make when it comes to encouraging their teen to continue reading is that parents stop reading to their teen. It's commonplace to see parents reading to younger children, even in public places. How many times have you seen a parent reading to a teen in the library? The first assumption would be that the teen is illiterate if an adult/parent is reading to him/her. On the other hand, it may be embarrassing for the teen to have a parent read to him/her in a public space.

Therefore, I encourage parents to read aloud to their teen at home. Perhaps you can read an article aloud or a poem. When I taught a high school writing class, we discussed poetry. I brought a book of Muhammad Ali's lyrical rhymes to class and read that aloud to the students. They enjoyed it because of Ali's witty, clever style of braggadocio. While the students may have known him well as a boxer, this was a new way to appreciate his artistry.

Parents often express to me that they cannot get their teen to read. That can be difficult if reading is competing with the television or a PlayStation. With my children, here's what I have done to encourage more reading:

- Enforce no TV watching on Monday through Thursday between school and bedtime.
- Have them attend teen events at the local library.
- Have a "reading" night at home.
- Discuss books/articles that I am reading.
- Recommend books to my teens.
- Hang out together in bookstores on the weekends.
- Attend book events where authors read excerpts from their own works.
- Listen to radio programming about books.
- Watch authors on TV.

What else would you add to this list? What have you tried with your teen? Please email me at drpamela@theeducationdoctor.com. Because of this reading foundation that my children had, they all love reading and actually still have friendly reading competitions.

I recently found the website teenreads.com which celebrates and reviews books for teens in a fun way. It's a great site that can encourage readers and non-readers.

Enjoy Meals Together

What is the single biggest predictor of better achievement scores and fewer behavioral problems for children ages 3-12? Having meals with their families. Eating together as much as possible builds strong family bonds that can help prevent risky behaviors such as experimentation with drugs, alcohol, and sex. (See challengesuccess.org for more study details.)

While it can be time-consuming and challenging to coordinate schedules around having meals together, the extra effort to prioritize this family time will pay dividends in the future. I accomplished this with my own family with these two practices:

1) Plan meals ahead for the week. I'm the primary cook for my family. The less time it takes to prepare a meal, then the less of a burden it would be to do so, especially after work. Planned menus save me time. Likewise, when I traveled on business, I would prepare entrees to refrigerate and post the menu for the week on the refrigerator so that my family could continue this tradition even in my absence. Having a menu limits the excuse to go out to eat or skip meals altogether.

2) Set boundaries for the television. One of the key rules on weekdays during the school year is no television allowed Monday through Thursday. To make it even more restrictive, there's only one television, which means that everyone has to agree on what to watch.

Build Strong Study Habits

Strong study habits are imperative to successfully navigate the high school years. If your teen is already practicing those strong skills prior to high school, then kudos to them. If not, then parents can play an active role in helping their teen establish strong study habits. Here are two quick ways to get started:

1) Find a good study space–This can be at home or away from home.

- **Options at home** may include the dining room table, a den, attic, garage, or basement.

- **Options away from home** may be a local coffee shop or even the lightly trafficked corner of a nearby library.

Sprawling on the bed or sitting cross-legged on the family room floor with the TV blasting the latest episode of *Family Guy* is probably not conducive to good study habits. Consider, though, that your teen may study best with music in the background–and it may not be the music you prefer. Music with lyrics may be distracting. If you don't think the music your teen is listening to encourages concentration, try gentle classical music, spa music, ocean sounds, or white noise like the sound of a fan or a radio dialed between stations. Other features of a good study place include a clear work area and ample lighting.

2) Set regularly scheduled study times. Work with your teen to commit to study times and stick with them. For lengthy periods of study, encourage your teen to take frequent breaks, perhaps, alternating thirty minutes of concentration with a few minutes of stretches. This can help restore previously high concentration levels. Students should make a note of where they were and what they were doing before the break so that they can quickly resume studying where they left off. (See bonus section of Chapter 5 for more study tips in "Tips to Ace High School".)

Apply A+ Attitudes™ Before High School

In Chapter 1, I introduced the A+ Attitudes™ that inform the success my programs have had with helping teens get into their top choice colleges and also garner significant scholarship awards. Those principles are as follows:

- A+ Attitudes™ #1 - It's All About Fit
- A+ Attitudes™ #2 - There's a Lot of Money Out There
- A+ Attitudes™ #3 - Distance Doesn't Matter

Even prior to high school, these attitudes can be applied to inform the decisions you make for and with your teen.

The remainder of this chapter demonstrates how you can apply these attitudes to make informed decisions that will build on the foundation you have set for your teen's educational journey.

Know Your High School Options

I urge parents to choose their teen's high school wisely and intentionally as it can strengthen their foundation and set the course for college and beyond. Early in your teen's middle school years (and maybe before), you should start to seriously consider which high school your child will attend. Some schools have waiting lists as well as extensive application and testing processes.

Here is an overview of the types of high schools that you may consider:

Day High Schools

Day high schools are schools that students commute to on a daily basis. This is the type of school that most high schoolers attend. In fact, they are so popular that some parents may not think of any other option. A day high school can be either public or private. They can have special programs such as performing arts, sciences, or college prep.

But the primary criterion for inclusion in this category is that the school does not offer on-campus housing for students.

Boarding High Schools

Boarding high schools make on-campus housing available to students. For some schools, the number of "boarders" can be at or near 100% of both students and faculty living in on-campus housing. Boarding schools have a complete residential community, including study time, extracurricular activities, and athletics all in one place with transportation for off-campus activities provided by the school. Some boarding schools incorporate travel abroad and a wide selection of Advanced Placement courses and the International Baccalaureate (a rigorous academic program that is globally recognized as the gold standard in high school curriculum).

In years past, the perspective on boarding schools was that parents would "send" their children there, sometimes against their child's wishes. Today, boarding schools are seeing a reversal in reputation. Teens are readily exposed to information about boarding schools through the internet and friends. As such, teens are now asking their parents to consider boarding schools for them. In my experience of working with families to find a boarding school that matches their teen's needs and interests, the parents typically had no prior experience or knowledge of boarding schools until their teen mentioned wanting to go.

I first learned about boarding schools when one of my middle school classmates in Memphis attended Phillips Andover Academy through A Better Chance, Inc. Through the years of attending college and graduate school, I met more students who had attended a boarding school and there was always a bit of mystique about their experiences. I really never gave much thought to my own children attending boarding school. It was hard enough for me to let them go to a day school after homeschooling so boarding school was almost unheard of until...

As an important aspect of my role in helping families find that best-fit high school, I visit high schools on a regular basis. It only took a few boarding school visits for me to realize that it's a truly unique experience. Boarding schools offer an intense and interactive experience with teachers and administrators that cannot be easily replicated in a day program. When I saw all the resources available in the boarding school environment, it opened my eyes to the possibilities for my own children. As I stated earlier on, parents want more for their children. Seeing what the boarding school environment could offer for my teen's development, I couldn't hold them back because of my fear of "letting them go."

Should you choose the boarding school option as my family did, you will want to prepare well in advance by researching schools and visiting campuses.

Specialty Programs

A huge trend in secondary schools is special programming which is offered within a day school or boarding school setting. I appreciate the special program models because they, in effect, recognize that not every student has the same learning needs or academic interests.

Here are several special programs worth highlighting so that you may consider whether one is a good fit for your teen:

- STEM (Science, Technology, Engineering, Mathematics).
- College prep.
- Learning or emotional focus.
- Single gender.

STEM (Science, Technology, Engineering, Mathematics)

There has been a growing interest in STEM education fields since reports have highlighted the high demand for jobs in Science, Technology, Engineering, and Math. Although schools have made strides to provide academic programs in STEM, they are required to collaborate more in their communities to find resources. Schools have been able to do science, technology, and math in a large part on their own. However, for the engineering curriculum, schools must often rely on the support of local industry and professionals to educate teens interested in this area of study. I visit dozens of high schools year round and rarely see the "E" in STEM being executed. For the "T" in STEM, schools are offering some support through advanced placement courses or school-based clubs. More communities are taking on the "T" through after-school initiatives, summer camps, and professional associations.

College Prep

College preparatory refers to those campuses that emphasize a core curriculum that prepares students for a 4-year college or university. Many of them may also have college prep options such as AP (Advanced Placement) courses or an IB (International Baccalaureate) program. Some college prep schools are public and may be magnet programs with lottery-based admissions in major urban areas such as in Chicago or New York. Sometimes, areas, such as suburban communities, are zoned as college prep.

Although high schools may have the label of college prep, they are not all created equal. Your teen may have to test in, particularly if the school is private, by taking an SSAT (Secondary School Admission Test) or ISEE (Independent School Entrance Examination), if public, state or national standardized achievement scores may be required.

One of the more controversial ways to get into a college prep program is through "tracking." Tracking occurs when students are channeled into certain courses based on their overall achievement and only attend classes with students of similar profile. This may seem like a good idea. Oftentimes, parents may not even be aware that their teen is being tracked until they learn that their student "can't get into" a certain class. Tracking begins in middle school, which is why it's so important to understand the projection of your teen's courses through high school.

On the opposite end, a teen can be tracked if they have a written IEP (Individual Education Plan) which outlines any special learning issues, such as hearing impairment, development delay or emotional disorders. In these cases, the special education teacher may have to sign off on course selection and students may be limited from taking any college prep courses, even if they are capable. The courses taken on either track will limit a student's college list in irreversible ways, which I will discuss further in later chapters.

Special Learning Needs

If your teen does learn differently, there are some schools that specialize in supporting such students. Those learning differences can range from dyslexia, dyscalculia (difficulty in learning math), ADHD (Attention Deficit Hyperactivity Disorder), to emotional disorders. This is why testing in middle school years is important so that your teen can be placed in the right school for them. High school can be a tumultuous time even under the best conditions, so the appropriate high school placement gives your teen the necessary support to be successful.

Single Gender Education

There is a growing movement around the benefits of single gender education. Some public schools have been allowed to have single gender classrooms or are single gender schools. There are private schools that have this approach as well as parochial schools. Studies have shown that girls are more likely to perform better in math and science in a single gender environment. Likewise, for girls, social issues may be less prevalent. For boys, single gender schools are tailored in a way to support how they learn, i.e., perhaps offering a physical activity before academic study. The primary thrust of the single gender movement is that the best learning environment where students can be most successful is the one that recognizes that girls learn differently than boys and vice versa.

Choose the Right Fit for High School

As you consider the best high school for your teen to attend, it starts with "fit" for your teen - academic, social, vocational, and financial fit. To understand how to make this premise actionable for your own teen, I will start with five key questions to ask when considering a high school for your teen. I will provide more detail for each to help with your choices.

1) How can this school support my teen academically?

Different schools may offer varying levels of support for the way your teen needs to learn. For example, your teen may be exceptionally bright and could benefit from a curriculum that offers accelerated courses or opportunities to take college-level courses during junior or senior year. If your teen has a special need such as dyslexia, then perhaps a high school with a strong learning center and a dedicated reading specialist may be a better match. Whatever your teen's academic needs, there is very likely a high school to meet those needs.

2) How is the school socially?

It's hard to know what a school is really like socially until your teen spends time there. Prior to making a decision about a school though, you can talk with other parents of the prospective high school. Find ways to connect your teen to other teens who attend that school. There are always several parents and students who can answer this question about the social vibe. If you don't know any parents of that high school personally, you may contact a leader in the parent organization as a start. Likewise, you could talk with a parent of a recent graduate.

There may be published sources, such as a weekly e-zine or school newspaper which will offer signs of what the social atmosphere is like. Additionally, as part of federal or state compliances, many public schools administer climate surveys. The survey discloses information about the culture of the school including beliefs and attitudes surrounding drug use, dating, stress, and bullying. The school can provide you with the survey results.

3) How will my teen's social needs be met?

Every parent wants his/her kid to be happy. At no time is this sentiment more felt than during the teen years. The social needs through the teen years are critical. Teens themselves want to fit in and be liked by peers.

As my daughter approached high school, I wrestled with the question, "Would she fit in and be liked by her peers in high school?" She had always attended a small K-12 school. Although she had many friends who would remain at the same school during high school, the size of her class just didn't seem that it would give her the social outlets she wanted. The question in my daughter's case became, "Which high school could offer a Black teen girl the best opportunities for her to flourish with peer and adult support, and hopefully, fewer tears?"

4) How has the school done in the last five years?

The local Department of Education publishes academic outcomes (the skills, knowledge, and abilities that students develop through their course work and other educational experiences) for all schools within their respective state. Be sure to look at the scores relative to your teen's needs and grade levels. When I sought this information for my own children, I reviewed the academic results for the current grade plus the grades ahead to see if there were any performance trends. As parents seek this data, there may even be information available for college placement test results for your review. These data points can assist with making the optimal decision for your teen.

5) What is the high school's college placement record?

A strong placement record indicates the degree to which a school is geared toward sending kids to college. Some schools may be labelled as "College Prep" but their program and college placement may vary widely from other similarly titled schools. You may be able to get these results from the school/college counseling office, district office, or department of education. When you do obtain the college placement records, notice which colleges are on the list and the percentage of students enrolling in the colleges. If more than 25% of the senior class is attending the same college, then that's a red flag for the level of attention and support that students are getting in developing their college list.

What Else to Consider about Academic Fit?

There are two things you will need to pay close attention to on the academic front as well. They include:

1) Math placement

2) Cognitive evaluations

We'll discuss each, in turn.

• Math Placement

There's been a lot of discussion among educators about math placement in middle school. More specifically, the math placement in middle school is where "tracking" begins. (Tracking refers to a determined path for the classes a student will take through high school.) When students are placed in an algebra course by 8th grade, it helps to establish their path to take accelerated and honors courses through high school. For example, here's a typical math pathway:

Grade 8 - Algebra 1
Grade 9 - Geometry (Standard or Honors)
Grade 10 - Algebra 2
Grade 11 - Trigonometry/Precalculus
Grade 12 - Calculus or AP Calculus AB

In this example, if a student is not enrolled in algebra by 8th grade, then the option to take an AP Calculus in his/her senior year will be a missed opportunity. Especially if a student is interested in a STEM major in college, math placement in algebra in 8th grade could predict their chances of college admissions in a STEM major.

Let me elaborate on what I mean by this... Many colleges will set a specific course of study as admissions criteria. For example, Carnegie Mellon University lists these courses as requirements for admissions to its College of Engineering and School of Design in College of Fine Arts:

College of Engineering

- 4 years English
- 4 years Mathematics*
- 1 year Chemistry
- 1 year Physics
- 1 year Biology
- 2 years Foreign Language
- 3 electives

School of Design

- 4 years English
- 2 years Mathematics
- 2 years Science
- 2 years Foreign Language
- 6 electives

Remember that colleges want to admit students who will thrive and contribute to their campus experience. The rigor of a student's high school curriculum shows the college how well a student may achieve academically at their institution.

There is a national push to have students take algebra in the 8th grade. The wisdom behind this seems to be that students who take algebra in 8th grade are more likely to go to college. There is controversy around these findings, however, with some arguing that students who take algebra as 8th graders are strong math students anyway and have excelled in the subject since 3rd grade. Hence, according to this viewpoint, they are more likely to go to college, just as they are more likely to win the Nobel Prize!

Regardless of the validity of the research or which side you take, if your teen is ready to take algebra in 8th grade, he/she should. Students who take algebra in 8th grade are poised to enter college prep and AP classes. One interesting statistic that I heard from an admissions officer at a major public university was that 80% of admitted students had five years of math. This means that the 80% admitted had algebra by 8th grade.

What if your teen isn't ready? It's not a good idea to push a student into algebra who is still struggling with basic math, like multiplication, division, fractions, decimals, rounding, and place values. In the name of equity for all, some schools are doing just that. This really does your teen a disservice if the push into algebra is not accompanied by support and additional instruction. Even still, teens learn at different rates and in different ways. If your teen has lagged behind in math since early elementary school, it is doubtful that this will change in Algebra I.

Talk to your teen's math teacher and counselor. Do this in sixth grade or as early as possible. If additional tutoring would help, there are numerous options ranging from school-based programs to private, one-on-one assistance. Ultimately, if your school's policies prohibit your teen from being on the college prep track without taking 8th grade algebra, you may have to accept it or find another school. But, either way, stay informed so that you know your teen's options.

• Cognitive Evaluations

In order for your teen to have the best chance for success in high school, it is important that you identify barriers to learning sooner rather than later. Armed with this information, you can make better strategic decisions about the type of high school that will be best for your teen.

If your teen struggles in school and you have no clear explanation of why, you may want to consider an independent neuropsychological evaluation prior to or during high school. A neuropsychological evaluation is conducted by a doctoral-level, licensed psychologist. The evaluation uses a series of clinical interviews and testing that, for the teen, mimics the school day. The intent is to see what the teen is like over an extended period, like 6+ hours. The test will include intellectual testing, memory, learning, visual-spatial, and motor skills. Throughout the day, the psychologist will also informally observe the teen's attention span, ability to focus, and response to distractions. Further, they listen to how your teen communicates and notes any tendency to go off on tangents, speak compulsively, or fidget in a developmentally inappropriate way.

The school assessment, as an alternative, is often limited in scope. Schools may test your teen if his/her teacher feels that he/she is unresponsive to traditional teaching methods. The purpose of this school assessment is often to find a more effective instructional approach. According to a pediatric neuropsychologist that I interviewed, schools are focused on creating an effective learning environment. This is great for the school, but may not be the best thing for your teen. This pediatric neuropsychologist added, "School evaluations are focused on the skills needed to achieve academic success but not on the psychological or medical assessment of the teen."

It is important that parents take a proactive approach and seek an outside evaluation in order to best serve their teen's needs. One of my client families had their teen assessed through a full neuropsychological evaluation and found that the teen had ADHD. The numerous assessments at school, however, did not pick up this finding.

Your teen may also be able to get special SAT (Scholastic Aptitude Test) or ACT (American College Testing) accommodations if a cognitive evaluation is already in place. Refer to each test site for the specific guidelines for accommodations. When I have assisted my client families with applying for accommodations, we start months ahead of the first test day. These accommodations may take months to finalize.

Remember that learning differences can be genetic. If you or your spouse or one of your other family member has reading, spelling, or other attention-based disorders, they are highly inheritable, according to neuropsychologists that I interviewed.

You are the primary advocate for your teen, learn as much as you can about the results of the evaluation so that you are clear in your communications to others. There is no reason to let your teen flounder. Learning differences are more common than most people think.

What About Paying for High School?

Scholarships to attend private high schools can come from one of three places: 1) directly from the schools, 2) local community-based organizations, or 3) a national program.

Most private schools provide financial aid scholarships based on need and/or merit. They may use the School and Student Services (SSS) documents of the National Association of Independent Schools, a member organization that represents the majority of private U.S. schools, to determine need. You would need to complete the Parents Financial Statement (PFS), an online form used by the SSS to determine your contribution. The decision on how much aid to award is solely the school's responsibility. Each school makes a determination based on the PFS analysis, the amount of available money, and whatever other criteria they use as determiners. It could be that they need a trombone player for the band, or that they are trying to expand their representation of a certain minority. It is crucial that you meet all deadlines for financial aid applications.

There are an increasing number of organizations that offer scholarships to teens attending private schools. They may be difficult to find at first and would require some sleuthing and lots of emails and phone calls to organizations in your area. For communities that do offer scholarship programs, the students are often first generation, low income, or diverse students. These community-based agencies work directly with the schools to negotiate financial awards for students that they recruit to that private school. The private schools benefit because: 1) They can diversify their student body, and 2) The agencies will provide additional support to help that student be successful during high school.

Here are a few well-known community-based organizations that offer financial assistance for high school:

- Oliver Scholars
- LEAD Chicago
- Prep for Prep, New York City

If you live outside of these areas, I would suggest reviewing these websites to find keywords that explain their program. Then, use those same keywords in an online search including your region or city name. This type of search may yield similar programs in your local community. In addition, you can ask other parents, teachers, and coworkers to refer local programs.

One national need-based organization that provides scholarships which can be used at participating private schools is A Better Chance, Inc. (ABC). A classmate from my middle school over thirty years ago had attended Phillips Andover Academy, a New England boarding school, through ABC, so it's a well-established program. Since then, several of my students that I have worked with privately are ABC students who attended day and boarding schools.

Bonus

High School Selection Checklist

NAME: _____   DATE: _____

Use this checklist as a quick guide for what to know prior to visit, observations during visit and relevant questions to ask:

- ☐ Academic Program (matches with your teen's needs or not)

- ☐ Teaching method (lecture, experiential or other that matches with your teen's needs)

- ☐ Activities available outside of class (based on your teen's interests or options to pursue)

- ☐ Students and families (peers, potential for friendships and opportunities to meet their families)

- ☐ Alumni support (are alumni actively involved and supportive?)

- ☐ Reputation (quality of reputation in the local community)

- ☐ Size (average classroom size and total enrollment for 9-12)

- ☐ Location (convenient for commuting or access to school bus)

- ☐ Cost of attendance (tuition, fees, activity participation, uniforms, lunches, field trips et al)

- ☐ Environment (feel of the school during visit, level of parent involvement, access to teachers after class)

- ☐ College admissions (where have students been admitted in prior 3 years)

- ☐ Application procedures (steps to apply and deadlines)

Next Steps/Questions: _____

_____

Pamela Ellis, The Education Doctor®, has helped thousands of teens attend a college that feels like home. She brings 25 years of experience in education to assist with college selection, admissions, financial aid, and freshman transition success. Dr. Pamela holds a PhD from Stanford and MBA from Dartmouth. For more tips and tools for college-bound teens, visit compasscollegeadvisory.com.

Chapter 3
Rethink Summertime

My oldest child went to his first sleep-away program in the summer after 4th grade. If you're thinking that 4th grade is "too young" to go away in the summer, I've heard that many times before. And I certainly could sense that other parents questioned my judgment at the time.

I had reviewed the program for months ahead of his applying and saw that it was well-established. Based on my research and goals for his summer, I figured that this particular program would be a safe, trusted environment where he could meet new friends, have fun, and keep up his academics in the summer. I talked with my son about it beforehand, of course, as there was an application process, even at that age.

For my family, personally, the 4th grade was very important as I was well aware of the research on Black boys which showed a sharp academic drop-off around that age. The goals I set for his summer experience were part of my effort to keep him engaged and excited about learning.

Summers present a wonderful opportunity to build upon the previous school year in a low-pressure learning environment. Your teen can explore an old interest or discover a new one. Summer also allows the time to hone skills, such as leadership, social negotiation, and creativity. There are free and low-cost summer activities in many communities.

At the same time that the summers may present enriching experiences, there are also opportunities for detrimental experiences. Research consistently shows that teens engage in risky behavior more frequently during idle times like the summer. That risky behavior can include drinking, drugs, sex, the wrong crowd, and countless other ways bored and curious teens can find to occupy long summer days. The need for social acceptance can lead an otherwise responsible teenager to pull some rather irresponsible stunts. These lapses in judgment tend to be more common in the teen years, but when coupled with too much idleness, unsupervised time when school is out can be a big problem for parents.

The good news is, however, that with so many options for summer engagement, there is no reason your teen should simply "hang out." This is not to say that students don't need some down time; they do. In fact, in my practice, I encourage students to have at least four weeks of time during the summer to "just be a teen." My students have used this "just be a teen" time for family travel, reading, volunteering, and spending time with siblings.

Start with the Goal in Mind

Summer is a great time for college-bound students and important enough that teens should be productive during their "off time." Although I'm not suggesting that the entire summer is filled with activities, I do recommend that your teen has 1-2 significant activities in the summer. What those 1-2 activities may be is based on who your teen is and what his/her goals are. Each year, when I'm working with teens, they do a couple of assessments, and we talk candidly about their short and long-term goals. I encourage you to have those same conversations as it relates to the summer and you and your teen working together on how your teen will spend the summer. Another thing we do is look week by week as to how the summer will be spent. You can do the same, and I suggest that you post a summer calendar on your fridge or someplace where your teen can easily see it and plan ahead.

To determine what your teen should do in the summer, you and your teen must set 1-2 goals, as it will help them to *be intentional* in considering the best use of their talents and time. As a guide to framing how to set specific, relevant goals for the summer, here's a grade-by-grade approach:

- Rising 9th—Transition into high school
- Rising 10th—Explore a new topic
- Rising 11th—Discover more about a field of study or career interest
- Rising 12th—Connect with colleges

Examples of summer goals may include:

- Meet new friends from around the world.
- Read five new books on topics that interest your teen.
- Take a course not offered at school.
- Learn more about a career in _____.
- Give more community service hours.
- Experience living away from home.
- You name it.

I group these goals into four larger categories (Reading, Writing, Volunteering, and Employment) that describe more how the summer can be crafted to meet your teen's needs.

Reading

My favorite summertime activity delivers a greater return on time spent than any other (more bang for your buck)... and that is reading... If you have access to a library, a computer, or even yesterday's newspaper, it's easy and free. Whether your teen is a self-proclaimed reader or not, parents have a role in promoting reading as a desired interest. Encourage your teen to read, read, and read some more. A great way for parents to encourage their teen to read is by reading themselves. You may have heard that saying that "kids are watching you at all times." Actions speak louder than words. If you are a reader, your teen may adopt the habit, as well.

For the teen who "hates" reading, challenge them to find something new. Everything counts, including the Sunday comics and *People* magazine. If your teen is struggling to find what to read, you may want to check out teenreads.com. Here are some additional quick tips to nudge your teen even more:

- Introduce your teen to more substantial reading material such as biographies of sports heroes, a business title, travel magazines, science fiction, or a book about his/her favorite hobby. One of my students was a very reluctant reader until he found a biography of Elon Musk. He was so interested in learning more about him that he read the hefty, 400+ pages in a week.

- Suggest a self-help book for teens, such as What Color is Your Parachute for Teens or Chicken Soup for the Teenage Soul.

- If your teen has trouble focusing while reading, select books that more fully engage the brain by including interactive exercises and activities. A book that my son read that he enjoyed is *Fluent Forever* by Gabriel Wyner. Your teen might like it too.

- Encourage your teen to ask for recommendations from people who love to read including other classmates, teachers, neighbors, and relatives.

- Have your teen join your local library's teen book club. Teens can sign up with their friends and support each other.

- Suggest that your teen spends an hour at the library scanning and familiarizing himself/herself with the Dewey Decimal System. This will be a way that your teen can learn how to find books in the library and also discover books that he/she may not have known he/she would be interested in.

- Make sure your teen has a dictionary handy to look up unfamiliar words. The actual book form of a dictionary is preferable to online dictionaries to avoid distractions such as email and social media.

The most important thing is for your teen to get to a point where he/she reads for enjoyment. Reading should never feel like an obligation. These suggestions offer a way for your teen to have a variety of topics and ways to enjoy reading. If none of these ideas work and your teen is concerned about testing well for college, you can let him or her know that the best way to improve his/her SAT score is through reading! Improved vocabulary as well as verbal and written communication skills are just a few side benefits.

Another benefit to regular reading is that readers may have an easier time with the summer program, scholarship, and college application process as well. Popular application questions include: "What book would you recommend for the freshman class and why?" or "What is the last book you read for pleasure?" If your teen enjoys reading and reads on a regular basis, then he/she will save a lot of time on writing his/her essay response to these prompts!

If your teen is already a reader and is interested in expanding his/her horizons, suggest that he/she starts reading some of the college preparatory classics. You can find lists online or through your local library. Many of the classics are available free in ebook format for Kindle, Nook, iPad, and other electronic readers.

When you notice that your student is reading, show interest but avoid lavish praise. Praise has a way of backfiring. You want your teen to enjoy reading for the intrinsic joy that reading provides, not because it makes you happy.

Writing

Whoever said that "Reading is fundamental" was "write"! Writing and reading go hand-in-hand but sometimes writing is shortchanged in its importance. Writing doesn't always have to refer to a school assignment, either. Journaling, for example, is another excellent summer activity. It helps students develop good writing skills as well as greater self-awareness. Furthermore, journals can help your teen deal with social situations, sadness, anger, or grief.

Journaling takes many forms. In addition to writing, journals may include other forms of self-expressions including poems, cartoons, drawings, collages, newspaper clippings, or small mementoes. One way that students can practice the skill of journaling is by keeping a travel journal. This can include travel ideas as well as actual travel and discoveries. In fact, one of my students kept a travel journal during her summer program experience, and it disclosed a gift in her that she didn't know she had, that of comforting others in need.

Free writing is a journaling technique that can help your teen if he/she is stuck on what to write. Using this technique, he/she simply writes for a specified period of time (or a specified number of pages), say ten minutes, about anything at all. It really doesn't matter what he/she writes. The point is to write in an uninhibited fashion without judgment or repression (nor concerns for grammar). Advice that I give to my own kids with free-writing is... head down, screen darkened, don't lift the pen from the paper. Free writing is a good exercise because it can help students overcome writer's block, express hidden emotions, and find a natural rhythm to their writing.

Writing is an art that students will continue to develop while in college. Getting comfortable with writing while in high school gives them the best chance of succeeding in their writing-intensive college courses.

Volunteering

Many teens want to do community service but
time for it during the school year. Summer is a great time to
expand on volunteer work. If your teen enjoyed a particular
volunteer activity previously, then encourage him/her to
continue with it through the summer. As a rule of thumb,
summer is a good time for 9th and 10th graders to try
something new. I recommend 11th and 12th graders
demonstrate consistency, if possible, by continuing to
volunteer in the same organization as in previous years. The
reason I suggest this is that continued experience may help
with letters of recommendation and expanded leadership
opportunities as they get older.

Of course, volunteering is its own reward in that it helps
to further an important cause or returns value to the
community. But, there are gains for the volunteer, as well.
Consistent volunteer work offers your teen the opportunity to
develop skills and share talents. Further, teen volunteers
experience many intangible benefits such as pride of
accomplishment, increased self-esteem, and a sense of
purpose—all good benefits during the sometimes turbulent
teenage years. Community service also affords teens the
opportunity to seek leadership roles and practice people
skills in a low-risk environment.

There are many non-profit, civic, and community
organizations that will appreciate your teen's talents. Some of
these organizations may be sources of future scholarships as
well. Your teen may seek to help at organizations like these:

- Churches, synagogues, mosques, and temples
- Shelters
- Food banks
- Congressional offices
- Political campaigns
- Conservation/environmental groups.

- Animal shelters
- After-school club

Teens can also find opportunities through the local papers and online at VolunteerMatch.org.

Working/Getting Paid

With the demands of coursework and extracurricular activities, students may find it impossible to work during the school year. Yet, work is a wonderful way to cultivate responsibility and independence in teens. Summer presents a good opportunity to get an age-appropriate job. You can guide the discussion by asking your teen what he/she hopes to accomplish by working. Certainly the occasional babysitting or lawn mowing gig will provide a little extra cash. However, with a little ingenuity, your teen can use a summer job to demonstrate leadership abilities and business acumen that will help him/her stand out from thousands of other "me-too" college applicants.

A budding entrepreneur can even start a business during the summer. The first step to starting up could be to research online how to set up the business, advertise it, and differentiate it from others offering the same service. In the case of a babysitting service, a teen could set up a service with two or more friends and advertise that the babysitters have taken the Red Cross Babysitter's training course or completed an online certification. A promotional idea may be offering group rates for three or more children. When my son expressed an interest in starting a business during the summer, I took him to a networking event to meet other entrepreneurs, and we took a marketing course together.

In addition to babysitting and lawns, teens can teach art classes for younger students, help at the community center, become a camp counselor, and find other creative ways to make money. Fiverr.com and similar web sites are communities of people willing to do small projects for a low fee, and there are teens selling their services, as well.

Some teens may want to pursue a job with an established business, perhaps a local restaurant or retail store. The process of applying for the job and talking to hiring managers is an invaluable experience that can help prepare teens for college interviews to come. But, even if they are not hired during the summer, they get good practice with interview skills and may be hired later on during school breaks.

An alternative to an actual job is to shadow an adult. The adult could be a parent, relative, neighbor, or anyone whose job accommodates shadowing. If your teen thinks he may be interested in a specific career, job shadowing is the opportunity to experience the position first hand and learn how to get there. You can help by encouraging your teen to be on the lookout for potential careers and asking appropriate questions. You and your teen do not have to figure out how the job shadowing will be structured in advance. Just ask. You never know what is possible until you ask. Your teen will not be able to scrub up for surgery or sit next to the Chairman in a sensitive board meeting, but there are many things he/she can do. You can help your teen initiate the conversation to request a shadow. This is good real-world practice in asking for what he/she wants and learning to tap into his/her available networks to get it.

Apply A+ Attitudes™ for Summer

The same principles I described for your teen prior to high school can also be applied as it relates to rethinking the summer:

- A+ Attitudes™ #1 - It's All About Fit
- A+ Attitudes™ #2 - There's a Lot of Money Out There
- A+ Attitudes™ #3 - Distance Doesn't Matter

You can think about summer programs as analogous to high schools, in that the summer program is determined by fit, there's financial aid available for summer programs, and it's OK if your teen gets an opportunity to live away from home!

If you're considering a summer program, here are key steps to find a program that best fits your teen's goals and interests.

Plan Ahead for the Summer

Summer should comprise a mix of enriching and varied experiences that are engaging for your teen while staying within your budget. It is likely that no one program will fill the entire ten-plus weeks of summer vacation, so you may want to plan for formal and informal programs. As my husband refers to it, you want to start with the "big rock first" which would be one formal program, then organize the summer calendar around informal programs/activities to fill the gaps.

Formal Summer Programs/Approach

A good option for reaching summer goals is to find a formal program. There are many types of formal programs in the summer that cater to a variety of interests and budgets. For grade school students, the price will generally differ between day programs (i.e. students commute to the program each day) and residential-based programs (i.e. students stay overnight at the program).

Beginning at around 4th grade, there are many more residential programs which increase in number for high school students. If a teen is considering college, then it's a good idea for him/her to experience a residential-based program during high school.

Academic and Non-academic Interests

There are academic and non-academic summer programs. Summer academic programs allow your teen to pursue his/her intellectual curiosity. Pre-college academic programs for high school students may include such subjects as creative writing, debate, or early history, as well as career-oriented programs in law, science, engineering, or pre-med. Non-academic pursuits may include video-gaming, sports, fine and visual arts, and music. Overall, summer programs also allow teens to build new skills, or increase confidence in something in which they already excel.

Community Service/Traveling Abroad

Whether the program features academic offerings or not, community service is becoming an increasingly popular component of summer programs. Community service is a non-academic pursuit that provides a rich summer experience. Students can also choose to study abroad, honing their culture skills and building upon a foreign language. I encourage students to consider these travel-abroad experiences as a complement to their in-school opportunities. For example, if a student is already studying French in high school, then a summer travel abroad experience to a French-speaking country could enhance their language skills further. This would especially be true if their high school doesn't already offer a travel abroad program.

Leadership Development

Leadership is a critical skill for students to develop as they prepare to enter college. Summer leadership programs can help to build confidence in the teen's unique talents and what he/she has to offer. For business-minded students, there are summer leadership programs incorporating collaborative group experiences or camp counseling younger kids. My younger son, Miles, for example, ran a simulated business as part of a summer leadership program in 8th grade. Further, there are experiential outdoor leadership programs like an Outward Bound or National Outdoor Leadership School.

Where to Look for Summer Programs?

There are five key ways to look for summer programs:

1) Conduct an internet search using specific keywords, based on your teen's summer goals. Let's say that your teen's summer goals are to meet new friends and learn about psychology (since it's not offered at school). An internet search with these terms could yield several options: "high school summer programs psychology pre-college " (You can add any state name if location matters).

2) Talk with other parents to find out about their experiences. However, listen with the caveat that whether a program worked or not for their teen, does not mean that it will be the same for yours.

3) Check the offerings of local day schools. Many independent schools have programs such as sports enrichment, tours, or travel. Some public schools may have programs as well, although the budget for such programs has been eliminated in many districts and/or may not be offered to "out-of-district" students.

4) Check private boarding schools in your state/region. Some may offer enrichment or skill-building programs to match your teen's goals. This could be an opportunity to experience living in a dorm, but in a high school setting surrounded by peers.

5) Research and contact colleges or universities. When you visit the institution's website, you may try searching with the keyword "high school" to find out what programs they offer. You may concentrate your search on colleges in the geographic area where your teen will most likely study. Keep in mind, however, that the summer programs are not necessarily affiliated with the undergraduate admissions office.

Therefore, admission to the summer program does not mean that your teen is a shoo-in for the college.

How to Find the Right Programs?

With so many choices for summer, you may be overwhelmed. To get a handle on identifying the best program for your teen, consider these three tips.

1) Start early. The summer program application process is fairly similar to the college application process in that it can be selective and take months to complete. The most competitive programs may even have January, February, or March deadlines. Therefore, I recommend looking into programs around October - December. Your teen may need to submit an application, essays, recommendations, graded assignments, and test results, if required, prior to the deadline. Once your teen has selected a program, then make sure he/she allows sufficient time to write the application and gather the application materials and supporting documents, such as teacher recommendations. Popular programs may fill quickly, so you may not have the flexibility to wait until June to find a program. Summer programs can range from free to $1,500+ a per week. Many programs may offer financial assistance so definitely inquire. In most cases, there are earlier deadlines to apply for any financial assistance, since funds are usually distributed on a first come basis.

2) Consider who your teen is to help him/her determine goals for the summer. A summer goal may be to learn a language that's not currently offered at high school, improve math skills, gain experience in a research lab, or learn how to live

with a roommate at a residential-based summer program. The key is understanding your teen's interests, needs, and maturity level. Talk openly with your teen so that you can both discover the type of experience he/she wants to have during the summer. Remember our objectives by high school year (pre-9-launch, pre-10-explore, pre-11-discover, pre-12-connect) as you refine the goal. There are dozens of programs available, so you will need to have clearly defined goals to avoid wasting time online searching.

3) Get Informed. Learn as much as you can about the programs that your teen is interested in. Contact the program staff and ask for family references in your area. Be sure to talk to a few references to get different perspectives. If, during your discovery, you find that the program staff is non-responsive or difficult, heed the warning. You are entrusting the staff with your teen and need to feel confident about the staff's leadership.

How to Create DIY Summer?

If you don't want to pay for or can't afford to have your teen participate in a formal academic program or travel, your family can put together your own summer program. It's important that you collaborate with your teen on this as you want him/her to like, enjoy, and keep up with this program. There are a number of ways to do this, including:

- **Online courses:** Self-directed independent learners may enjoy taking online courses during the summer. However, pay attention to quality as it can vary widely, and cost may provide little indication of substance. The course should have an instructor who is qualified in the subject and able to provide help should your teen have issues. My kids personally prefer Khan Academy and Coursera. There should be technical assistance to work through computer or administrative problems. There are also Advanced Placement (AP) courses offered in the summer (either online or offline.) However, the AP exams are not administered until May. This leaves a long gap over which to forget the material. In any case, your teen can check with collegeboard.org to ensure that the course is authorized. Additionally, remember to have your teen check with his/her high school to be sure he/she will get credit for AP or other summer course(s).

- **Online games:** There are many academic games available online such as those on mathforum.org, coolmath.com, and freerice.com. Freerice.com is owned by the United Nations World Food Programme and is a site where you can earn 10 grains of rice with each correct answer. The rice is donated by sponsors to combat world hunger. This is a fun opportunity for a summer-long friendly competition between your teen and his/her friends.

- **Test prep:** Your teen might also consider doing ACT or SAT practice problems online, taking an ACT/SAT prep class, or working with a private tutor. While I strongly recommend that students only focus on one test, I also encourage students to take the test as close to their test prep as possible. Thus, if your teen is taking the ACT or SAT test in the winter, then summer prep may not be ideal.

- **Library or community reading programs:** Local libraries or community centers may have reading program for teens. If there isn't a reading program in your community, find one online to follow. Another option may be to find other students who want to participate in a reading group together.

- **College reading lists:** Check out reading lists for entering freshmen online. If the college reading list is too advanced, look for high school lists or tackle the classics.

- **Documentaries:** Many public libraries have documentaries that you can check out with a free library card. You can also find documentaries online or through Hulu, Netflix, PBS Video, or SnagFilm. Your teen can identify a topic of interest and watch several targeted films or simply watch what interests him/her the most. Your teen can combine the documentaries with journaling about the videographer's perspective and purpose, his/her own perspective, as well as family discussions about the video.

While the informal programs can save money, the challenge with cobbling together your own program is that unless you and your teen are extremely disciplined, life tends to get in the way. Just as with homeschooling, parents must provide the structure and support and hold the teen accountable for upholding the routine. Even the most motivated teen may resent parents for taking on this role. As I often state with caution to client parents, "Be the parent, not the teacher," and you'll be better off.

Bonus: The Education Doctor® Summer Program Favorites

This list is not exhaustive, but shows the types of programs available and can help you get started on finding the best summer program for your college-bound teen:

- Boston University RISE Internship/ Practicum
- COSMOS—California State Summer School for Math and Science
- Economics for Leaders
- High School Journalism Institute at Indiana University
- Johns Hopkins Summer Institutes
- Rhodes College Summer Writing Institute
- Phillips Exeter Academy Summer
- Summer Science and Engineering Program at Smith College
- The Debate Institute at Dartmouth College
- Washington University Summer Institutes

Part II
Navigating the
High School Years

Chapter 4
Look Forward

The middle and high school years are the best years to prepare for college success. In the previous chapters, I spoke about what you must know and do before high school. For my own kids, "before high school" began around 4th grade, with my being intentional about their school experiences during the school day, their after-school activities, and how their summers were spent. I realize that you may be reading this book long after those early years, and if this is the case, I want you to still feel encouraged that you can help your teen achieve his/her educational vision of college and beyond. Two ways to take action during high school is to 1) plan ahead for all four years of high school and 2) be intentional in each school year!

Stop Planning for Each School Year

To be both strategic and intentional about preparing for college success through high school, you must go far beyond planning 9th grade course work to planning how your teen spends summers and after school activities, earns spending money, preps for standardized testing, and develops relationships with peers and adults, including, of course, teachers. Part of this preparation includes knowing your teen and helping your teen know himself/herself and being okay with who he/she is. Pressure on teens to be what family, school, church, etc., expects them to be can backfire into unfortunate consequences.

Planning for high school a year at a time wastes time and positions your teen to have a reactive high school experience. The key to navigating the high school years towards college success starts with the "big rock" of academics... planning ahead for all four years of high school coursework at the start!

You can help your teen map out the courses for all the high school years. Doing so can help, but it is not necessary that your teen has an idea of the type of coursework he/she wants to take beyond the basics needed for high school graduation or to gain admission to any specific colleges. As a start, you and your teen can check your state's department of education website for specific suggestions on college preparation standards, required exit examinations, and/or admission to the state's flagship institutions. This research will assist you and your teen in planning ahead and eliminating any senior year surprises.

A standard college-bound schedule may include these courses in each of the four years:

1) Math, including Algebra I and II, Geometry, and Trigonometry, or Calculus

2) English or literature, with an emphasis on the more traditional classes, such as American literature and college preparatory classes such as expository writing.

3) Science, including Biology, Chemistry, and Physics.

4) Social Science, including U.S. and World History, U.S. Government, Geography, and Economics, if available.

5) Foreign language, preferably only one language that is continued throughout high school years.

Skimping on this basic curriculum can limit your teen's college options and potentially limit future job choices since these high school choices could strongly influence college majors.

A common question from parents about this recommended four-year plan is whether their teen can "get by" with three years of math, science, or social studies? My response is "Perhaps." Although your state high school graduation requirements may allow only three years in those subject areas, the colleges on your teen's list may require four years in each of the core areas. In my experience of working with college-bound teens, I've noticed that when students are applying to colleges for a STEM major, they will likely need all four years of English, math, science, and social studies. For one of my students interested in majoring in computer science, one of the colleges on her list, Carnegie Mellon, required a high school physics course. She was able to swap another science course in her senior year so that she could submit a competitive college application.

Foreign language courses in high school are also well worth pursuing for all four years of high school. When I am working privately with students and my own kids, I encourage them to stick with the same foreign language throughout high school so that it keeps their college list open. One of my students was very adamant that he did not want to take another year of Spanish in his senior year. Although he realized that one of his top choice colleges required four years of a foreign language during high school, he wouldn't budge. He even went so far as to include a letter in his application requesting a waiver for the foreign language requirement. If his high school didn't offer the course, I believe that the waiver letter would have been understandable. All the other aspects of his application were strong. However, he was denied admission. I believe that his denial was due largely to him not having four years of a foreign language during high school.

Some students tell me that they would prefer to take subjects that they are more interested in and forego some of the core requirements. That's fine, but keep in mind that admissions committees look for sufficient rigor in the high school coursework. Even if your teen's high school has limited course offerings, your teen should still take the most rigorous courses offered and perhaps consider summer school or summer programs as a supplement. Your student is only expected to take what is available to him. However, if your teen attends a college preparatory high school and shuns rigor in favor of personal interests, they may suffer the consequences of not getting in or not getting money for college.

Beyond academics, additional activities should be planned out, especially if they involve significant time commitments for your family. My teens played with a chess club in another city which involved weekly travel during the school year. Because we prioritized chess, my teens did not participate in any activities that conflicted with chess club meetings or tournaments.

There is no shortage of ways that teens can be involved outside of coursework. Outside activities may include:

- City-wide competitions
- Civic groups
- Community service
- Foreign language clubs
- Religious activities
- Social clubs
- Sports
- Youth associations

These outside experiences provide students with a chance to try something new, meet new friends, and enjoy downtime. For some teens, the outside activities may help them in better managing their time.

With my older son, for example, I find that when he has to balance outside activities in addition to schoolwork, he prioritizes his schedule better. I guess the old saying holds true here... "When you want something done, ask the busy person."

One of the ways that I help my students get a sense for how they want to spend their time over the four years of high school is by having them prepare an activities resume at the beginning of 9th grade. I will share more about the activities resume in the next chapter and you can see a template.

Be Intentional Where You Are

As a parent, we all experience a bit of guilt at times, like we're not doing enough for our children or not spending enough time with them. I was reading a recent column written by an Ohio-based psychologist and one of the things he included on his list of "10 things that every parent should stop doing right now" was making "your child your highest priority". I'm certainly guilty of doing that at times which is why I feel bad when I forget to do something for my children. That "something" I forgot is often not that significant. What's most important, though, is that the "big rocks" get done!

I say all of this because I want you to feel encouraged in knowing that even if you haven't done all the things that are outlined in this book, you can still take action now to help your teen achieve success in college and beyond. These next chapters provide a guide for you to actively support your teen's success through high school. I'm a working mom, so I understand that you may not have the bandwidth to "do it all" and that life can get in the way of even the best intentions.

Each chapter is organized by year of high school, with the months of each year detailed. My hope is that this will make it easier for you to be able to take action wherever you are in the process. I think this is critically important because, as working parents, we can often feel like we're not doing enough.

Chapter 5
Freshman Year (Self-Aware)

The freshman year of high school can be daunting as so much about how your teen "does school" suddenly changes. In my practice with high school freshmen, we do not even talk about colleges... they hear enough of that at home and at school. My primary focus with freshmen is nurturing their self-awareness. I want students to get to know their own likes and dislikes, strengths and shortcomings. Ninth grade is an ideal time for this focus as students can, in a sense, recreate themselves when they start high school.

I administer assessments to the students to give us a common language and way of initiating conversation about them without any awkwardness. At the end of this chapter, noted in the bonus section, are a few assessments that you can give to your teen at home.

Expect a Social Transition in the Freshman Year

Plenty of research shows that the freshman year is the most difficult.

The freshman year is a year of learning about self–a year of self-awareness. Think of the freshman year as the orientation to your teen's educational journey. I refer to it in this way because the freshman year is a time when teens can chart a course for the future, whether it ends in high school, college, or graduate school. My hope is that what starts in the freshman year of high school is an orientation to lifelong learning, not just high school.

With both academic and social challenges facing freshmen, the 9th grade can be a stressful year. There's certainly a lot more pressure academically in the freshman year as grades and courses start to "count" in a way that they may not have been counted in middle school. Academic rigor usually increases from the middle school curriculum. Although grades count in 9th grade, your teen still has an opportunity to figure out what his/her interests are, and course corrections can be made next year. Getting to know the teaching styles of new teachers may also play a role in the academics being "harder."

The biggest adjustment in the freshman year, however, is the social transition. There are so many influences from peers, and, not to mention, parental expectations. From a social standpoint, students are trying to navigate a new environment and new groups of students with new kinds of social and communication dynamics. Their peer relationships become increasingly more important than parents, and sometimes, even the values that their parents have taught. Girls may often feel this peer pressure more so than boys. This social transition was particularly challenging for my daughter and I have experienced it with my female clients, more than with my male clients. In short, girls can be petty, cliquish, and catty in a way that interferes with doing well.

With the increased role of technology in our teen's lives, today there are higher rates of cyberbullying than ever before, with 26% of girls vs 17% of boys experiencing such behavior. (Data taken from a Cyberbullying Research Center study at cyberbullying.org.) This is exacerbated by the negative self-view that can start to emerge as students transition to high school. If students are going to drop out, either physically or emotionally, 9th grade is most likely when it happens. (See Camille A. Farrington's book, *Failing at School*, for more insight on the 9th grade.)

Schools are beginning slowly to recognize these transition challenges. There are some school districts that have created summer bridge programs to ease the transition between 8th and 9th grade. This allows time for kids to bond before the start of the school year. There are also math or other academic review programs, prior to the first day of freshman year.

Whether your school district offers such a bridge program or not, parents can look into summer programs that provide the types of skills and attitudes that teens will need for a successful high school transition. These private programs for rising 9th graders can help your teen jumpstart the high school experience through meeting other rising freshmen and learning what to expect during high school. In my advising practice, I have recommended these types of summer bridge programs for teens who are starting a new school outside of their district (see bonus section at the end of this chapter). For specific skills development, students may consider investing in a study skills program or math review program through a tutoring organization.

In my experiences with students attending a K-12 school, i.e., lower, middle, and high school programs are on the same campus, there is still a transition in 9th grade which cannot be underestimated.

Apply A+ Attitudes™ in 9th grade

As a busy parent, you may not have the time to stay on top of all the ways you can support your freshman's success through high school especially when so much about high school has changed from the way you and I may recall it! It will always be the case, as well, that life does get in the way of all of our well-intentioned plans to "be there" for our children. Our teens still need us to parent, albeit in different ways. I believe that how we parent should be responsive to the teen's maturity, schooling, personality and life experiences.

This month-by-month guide to support your 9th grader's success during the academic year focuses on fostering self-awareness while recognizing the social transition to high school. I created this roadmap with the busy parent, like myself, in mind. I am the mother of three children, and it's a challenge to keep up with all the activities for each of them. From that perspective, I have kept this guide intentionally simple. If you have the time to do so, you may actively follow through on each task each month. If you don't have the time, then I encourage you to focus on your teen completing one action a month. The idea of this monthly guide is that it makes it easier on you in supporting your teen and reminds you with regular "to-dos." This guide is meant to be one that you can reference as needed to support your teen's success. It is NOT intended to be overwhelming, anxiety-raising, stressful, or anything like that. You can think of it as me "holding your hand" through this educational journey for your teen!

Role Check: Keep in mind that the action items are for your teen to actually do, and your role is to make sure they stay on track!

How to Do 9th Grade with Your Teen Month-by-Month

August

❖ **Together with your teen, set up an 8th grade roadmap for the school year.** See the sample roadmap in bonus section at the end of this chapter or you may download a printable version at this link: (theeducationdoctor.com/whattoknow). The printable road-map, from my website, includes one actionable tip for each month with space for you to add other events or actions throughout the year. When you provide an email address to get the printable roadmap online, you will also receive additional bonus tips throughout the freshman year to add to your teen's personal roadmap. Please remember to post the printed roadmap in a visible place so that your teen builds a habit of planning ahead and stays accountable.

❖ **Determine 1-2 goals for 9th grade year.** Based on reviewing the freshman roadmap and considering what your teen wants to achieve throughout high school, your teen should feel empowered to set 1-2 goals for this year. Examples of goals for 9th grade may be:

- Meet with math teacher two times per month to review problem sets and/or graded exams.

- Attend all meetings for one new co-curricular club.

- Earn 90%+ score in three core courses for the year.

- Achieve Honor Roll each term.

- Spend thirty hours volunteering with a community agency (make sure that it's an agency that your teen cares about).

❖ **Set up a filing system.** In addition to your teen setting up a file, i.e., in Google or Dropbox to keep online documents, also help them set up a simple, old-fashioned paper folder system. A paper system would include manila folders from an office supply store with labelled tabs. Only four or five folders are needed to set up the paper system. Your teen can choose among these labels for their file folders:

- Sample Essays

- Scholarships for College

- Honors and Achievements

- Co-Curricular Activities

- Basketball or Cross-Country or Football or Lacrosse, etc.

- Interesting Articles

- Testing for College

September

❖ **Confirm courses**. Review the course schedule for the entire year to ensure that the right classes are included. Make adjustments, if necessary, based on the four-year academic plan for your teen (as discussed in "Chapter 4 – Look Forward"). If there are conflicts, your teen may need to make adjustments such as adding a course during the summer or taking a course at a local community college.

❖ **Attend at least one social function, if offered.** Most school calendars will include a sporting event or dance early in the fall. This will be an opportunity for your teen to socialize with classmates and meet new students. If no school event is scheduled this month, then encourage your teen to spend time outside of school with one new friend in his/her class. (This is the high school version of a "play date.") The idea is that your teen is encouraged to nurture new friendships as they will do throughout high school and into college as well.

October

❖ **Increase class participation.** Now that your teen has had a chance to get more familiar with his/her teachers and subject areas, it's time to engage more in the class room. Class participation can include asking questions, volunteering for an activity, and/or commenting during discussion. In addition to asking your teen if he/she is speaking up in class, ask your teen's teachers about his/her participation in class.

❖ **Meet with teachers outside of class time.** A good habit for your teen is to meet with each teacher at least once during the term. Certainly, if there is a class where they want to get extra help from the teacher, then your teen can set a time to meet with that teacher more frequently. I encourage students to start developing these relationships sooner so that they learn the importance of self-advocacy and having a network of supporters.

❖ **Try a new club and/or co-curricular activity.** Now is the time for your teen to create new experiences and push outside any comfort zone. He/she will need an activities resume to complete his/her college application. (See sample activities resume in bonus section at end of this chapter.) The activities your teen participates in, however, should NOT be a bunch of meaningless activities just so your teen can say he/she was a "member" of a club. Admissions officers want to know the passion and interest behind a teen's activities and understand the impact these activities have on your teen and others. What better time to help your teen identify his/her passions than in this first year of high school. Then, as your teen's coursework becomes heavier and his/her time becomes scarcer, he/she won't find himself/herself running around looking for things to join. The quality of your teen's involvement is crucial. Encourage your teen to push outside the box. Your teen may be surprised at the new interests he/she identifies.

November

❖ **Check grade reports.** Depending on mid-term grades and teacher comments, your teen should use the teacher's feedback to keep doing well in subjects in which he/she is excelling. If grades are incongruent with the effort your teen has put forth, then it's a great time to consider more help. This may include getting a tutor, having your teen speak to the teacher about extra credit assignments, picking up a review book, or taking an online course.

Research scholarships. There are scholarships for college that your 9th grader may qualify to win. One of the websites your teen can search is unigo.com. Many of the scholarships may require an essay so make sure that your teen plans ahead to meet the deadlines. It's a good idea to post the deadlines on your family calendar at home and have your teen note the deadline in his/her phone calendar as well. If your teen finds a scholarship that's for the next school year, then be sure that your teen prints the description of that scholarship and adds it to his/her "Scholarships" folder.

December

❖ **Volunteer.** The holidays typically present a great time for teens to volunteer in the local community. My primary rule of thumb is that any volunteering must be done for an organization or cause that your teen cares about. Getting an early start in community service by 9th grade means that before your teen gets to a busy junior year of high school, he/she will already have about two solid years of involvement with the charity, gaining some real world work experience as well as developing relationships with community-minded adults.

January

❖ **Start researching/planning for summer.** The summer after 9th grade is a great time to explore a new topic. Oftentimes, 9th graders may not have any particular college major interests or know what they want to do when they "grow up." My son had several different interests as a 9th grader and had already attended a couple of STEM related summer programs. So when he and I researched summer programs for post-9th, we considered non-STEM programs. I would also strongly urge you to research programs early because scholarship deadlines are usually much earlier than the application deadlines. Summer programs can be expensive, so I always applied for scholarships.

❖ **Submit summer program applications.** The more popular summer programs may have a "rolling admissions" policy where students are admitted to the program until spaces are filled. If your teen is applying to a program with rolling admissions, then I highly recommend that your teen applies to these programs earlier, so they have the best chances of being admitted.

February

❖ **Monitor Facebook and other social media sites.** Now is a good time for your teen to learn more about his/her online footprint and begin to self-monitor his/her social media presence. I also encourage you, as his/her parent, to carefully monitor what your teen is doing online if you had not already been doing so. More and more colleges are on social media and your teen does not want to jeopardize his/her future because of inappropriate social media posting(s). Given the public and viral nature of social media, you can never know who's reading nor what the ramifications may be.

My suggestion to parents is that YOU should be connected to your teen on Facebook. In fact, your teen should be connected to both parents as well as other responsible adults who can monitor what goes on there. Your teen should monitor his/her social media accounts, other online activities, and beware of any inappropriate/questionable posts from his/her friends.

March

❖ **Research scholarships and deadlines (track in filing folder for "Scholarships").** Whether you completed this task during November or not, checking again for scholarships helps your teen to develop a habit of planning ahead for scholarship opportunities. Be sure your teen adds any upcoming deadlines to your family calendar (and on his/her smartphone) so he/she remembers to apply.

❖ **Determine courses for next year.** Typically, when I work with students enrolled in private, independent schools, they are required to submit course requests in the spring of the prior year. (This is likely the case because the teen's parents are also deciding whether to sign an enrollment contract for the next school year during this time.) Once the schedule for your teen's sophomore year is ready, I encourage you to review the courses with him/her to be sure that the courses still match with your overall academic goals and the four-year plan. My own children attended a private high school, so I would spend each spring going through their course schedules for the next school year. Each would select their courses along with their academic advisor, then I would review it with them to ensure that they would still be on track with their math and foreign language progress. I focused on math for each because I wanted them to keep their college options open regardless of their major. The foreign language was important for us because each studied Mandarin and we had selected their high school for that program. I certainly didn't want to make such an investment for them to attend this school for this opportunity, and they stop taking Mandarin. Studying math and Mandarin were my non-negotiables.

April

❖ **Finalize your summer calendar.** Summer programs will typically notify your teen by late March/early April of their admission decision. Be prepared to make a deposit right away if your teen is admitted to a summer program. Having one formal summer program in place will help with planning the other weeks of the summer. I will say again that every week of the summer does not have to be filled.

Your teen should have time to relax, enjoy time with friends, read, and just be himself/herself.

❖ **Stay on track with study plans for the AP exam.** Most high schools do not allow 9th graders to take Advanced Placement courses. However, if your freshman does qualify to take an AP course, make sure that they use this month to study well for the AP exams. Likewise, if they are taking any AP exam, please consider having them register for the corresponding SAT Subject Test. (See 11th grade month-by-month roadmap for more details on AP and SAT Subject Tests.)

May

❖ **Advanced Placement tests.** Your teen will take any AP exams during the first two weeks of May. You may go to my website and search for "AP test dates" to find the upcoming schedule for your teen.

❖ **Update activities resume.** Now that the school year has come to a close, it's a great idea to update your teen's 9th grade activities resume while it's still fresh in mind. Please remind your teen that any middle school activities should be removed. Updating the activities resume now will also help with determining summer goals.

June

❖ **Take SAT Subject Test(s).** These tests should only be taken if your teen took an AP course during 9th grade. If not, please don't worry that your teen is "missing out"... he/she is still on track for college admissions success!

❖ **Set your teen's summer reading.** As I discussed in "Chapter 2 – Prepare Before High School," reading for pleasure is key to getting into college and getting money for college. Your local library is a great resource for helping your teen find books to read this summer. The teen librarian can recommend age- and content-appropriate books for your teen and will likely have a summer reading challenge that your teen can participate in. Getting a head start on these summer reading challenges in 9th grade makes reading more fun and offers a place for your teen to make friends with other readers.

July

❖ Enjoy summer activities and keep on reading!

Bonus

Freshman Monthly Roadmap

In addition to this Roadmap to Get In Get Money™ for college, you will receive weekly update emails with additional real-time tips to add to this checklist. I would love to partner with you to achieve your teen's educational vision. Please contact me today - drpamela@theeducationdoctor.com

August
- ☐ Meet 1-2 new classmate(s)
- ☐ _____
_____

September
- ☐ Get comfortable with high school routine
- ☐ _____
_____

October
- ☐ Set academic and social goals
- ☐ _____
_____

November
- ☐ Get involved in 1-2 clubs at school
- ☐ _____
_____

December
- ☐ Volunteer for community activity
- ☐ _____
_____

January
- ☐ Meet with teacher(s) to overview 2nd semester objectives
- ☐ _____

February
- ☐ Apply to summer program(s)
- ☐ _____
_____

March
- ☐ Develop 4-year course plan with College Bound ReadiGuide™
- ☐ _____
_____

April
- ☐ Finalize sophomore courses
- ☐ _____
_____

May
- ☐ Set summer reading plan and calendar
- ☐ _____
_____

June: **This is your summer to "Explore"... Enjoy!**

Pamela Ellis, The Education Doctor®, has helped thousands of teens attend a college that feels like home. She brings 25 years of experience in education to assist with college selection, admissions, financial aid, and freshman transition success. Dr. Pamela holds a PhD from Stanford and MBA from Dartmouth. For tips and tools to help your college-bound teen, visit compasscollegeadvisory.com.

Copy and post this checklist to keep track of expectations and actions to navigate 9th grade year.

Bonus: Sample Activities Resume

123 SAMPSON ST • WINSTON, CA 94123
(408) 489-4608 • AGRAYSON@DOMAIN.COM
DOB: 05/05/2001

ALEX GRAYSON

OBJECTIVE

- College Major: Psychology, Spanish
- Intended Career: Physician

EDUCATION

- Washington High School, Winston, CA (8/2016 –Present)
- 3.67 *weighted* GPA
- Rank: 12/80
- Graduation: May 2020

ACADEMIC HONORS

- Honor Roll, 9th Grade Fall and Winter term
- National Math Honors Academy
- AP, Honors or Accelerated Courses Previously Taken:
  - 9th: Biology Honors, AP World History
  - 10th: Chemistry Honors, AP Government

PERSONAL STRENGTHS

- Curious
- Motivated
- Perseverant

CURRENT YEAR COURSES

- AP Government
- Algebra 2
- Chemistry Honors
- English 10
- Health and Wellness
- Music

Bonus: Sample Activities Resume (continued)

Activities, Volunteer, Clubs, Etc.	9	10	11	12	Accomplishments	Wks/Yr & Hours
Volunteering/Community Service						
Elementary School Reading Program	x	x	x		• Tutored students • Supervised new peer volunteers • 3 hours/week; 40 weeks/year	
School Athletics						
Varsity Basketball		x	x		• Led team in scoring each season • Selected as captain in junior year • 15 hours/week; 11 weeks/year	
Club Athletics (none)						
Clubs & Extracurriculars						
Student Government	x	x			• Elected to represent 9th & 10th Grade classes • Organized fundraiser that earned $1,000 for school supplies • 3 hours/week; 33 weeks/year	
Summertime Experiences						
OSU Summer Scholars – Columbus, OH			x		• Selected for rigorous pre-medicine, residential program • Shadowed physicians • Conducted research on tumors • 4-week program	
Employment						
Winston Lawn Services. San Jose, CA	x	x			• Mowed lawns and raked leaves • Started workdays at 6 am in summer • 8 hours/week; 35 weeks/year	

Bonus: Tips and Resources for Freshmen

Inventories/Assessments for Your Teen to Increase His/Her Self-Awareness

- Birkman
- Do What You Are
- Highlands Ability Battery
- Strengths Explorer
- Strong Interest Inventory

Summer programs

- Dana Hall Summer Leadership Program for rising 9th grade girls is a one-week residential program for girls to develop the skills and resources to enter high school.
- Center for Talent Development at Northwestern offers online, weekend, summer and assessment programs for talented students in middle through high school grades.
- Duke Talent Identification Program (TIP) offers online, year-round and assessment programs for talented students in middle through high school grades.
- Business Week is a high school business development program run during the summer in states across the US, including Ohio, Washington and Louisiana.

The Education Doctor® Podcasts

These podcast episodes are relevant for freshman year:

- "What Parents Must Know About Getting Money for College"
- "How to Help Your Teen Write Better"
- "How to Help Your Teen Improve Their Study Habits"

You can download at theeducationdoctor.com/whattoknow

Tips to Ace High School

These bonus tips are reflections from my son, Jan, who is an undergraduate at Georgetown University, School of Foreign Service.

❖ **Learn and practice good study skills.** If high school is easy for your teen and he/she rarely cracks a book, then make sure he/she takes the toughest classes from the toughest teachers. He/she needs to learn to study and should take notes in every class.

❖ **Review notes while they are still fresh and fill them out where needed.** For some students, just the act of writing notes down on paper is enough to secure them in long-term memory. For most students, however, a thorough review of the notes later ensures that they are prepared for the inevitable pop quiz, that they will have fewer marathon sessions at exam time, and, most importantly, that they get the most of each school day. Students will learn the material and remember it longer if they learn to study in high school. Granted, in high school, they may be called upon to do little more than read-and-regurgitate. That is, read the few pages the instructor tells them to read, scribble a few notes in class, listen closely at the test review sessions, and then cram the night before. They'll get by just fine, but they will not have learned much. Contrary to popular opinion around the halls of most high schools, cramming isn't learning.

Unfortunately, the ability to read-and-regurgitate may serve some students well in high school; it won't serve them at all in college. Why? They will be asked to read much more, the reading will be more complex, and no one is going to help them prepare for a test. If they fail to show up for every class, take copious notes, read and re-read the textbook as well as the supplemental reading materials, and review their notes each night, they probably won't do very well.

❖ **Organize class materials by subject–make to-do lists.** If your teen is not a natural list-maker and suffers from too much to remember, list-making is a skill that will serve him/her well. Your teen should write down everything he/she needs to do up to and including getting his/her homework off the printer and putting his/her backpack by the door. Teens have too many things to remember to rely on memory. Also, checking things off the list is gratifying. By doing so, your teen can see how much he/she has accomplished. Your teen should review his/her to-do list each morning.

❖ **Your teen should get to know his/her teachers and let them get to know him/her.** Your teen should develop good relationships with his/her teachers and inform them of his/her goals. Your teen will need great recommendations and the school counselor can be particularly helpful with scholarships, in addition to admissions.

Chapter 6
Sophomore Year (Explore)

The sophomore year is when students can "find' themselves. It's often considered as a "middle-child syndrome" year in that students are no longer the new kids at school and not yet getting the attention that juniors receive. If you think back to your 10th grade year, is there anything special that you remember about it? For my high school years, I remember 9th grade, the second half of 11th grade and 12th grade. There's nothing that stands out about 10th grade for me.

Even when I think back to my sophomore year of college, there's nothing that stands out. I recall my college roommates, Autumn and Debbie, and we still talk about the year that we lived together in a temporary trailer park on Stanford's campus, with the music of Janet Jackson's "Control" blaring. I also recall hearing the crisp sound of a CD player for the first time during my sophomore year of college. While there was a lot I remember socially about that year, I draw a total blank on the academic experience.

Sophomore year of high school is very similar in that regard. So as your teen goes through 10th grade, you can anticipate a bit of a "slump," but this year also presents a tremendous opportunity for your teen to explore who they are and want to become.

Beware of the "Sophomore Slump"

During the freshman year, your teen may have gotten a lot more attention as a new student. There may have been a new student orientation and even an assigned peer mentor. Now, as a 10th grader, there's a bit less fanfare and no more welcome activities. If your sophomore is attending a college prep high school, then your teen may see how the juniors are getting more attention from teachers and counselors with their college admissions process. In short, your sophomore may just feel more left out.

On the bright side of this school year, though, students have a chance to find themselves and explore under the radar because no one seems to be paying attention. They can try things out, if you will. If your teen hasn't already made a few close friends, then 10th grade can be a time to perhaps join a new group or get acquainted with a student who's not attached to a group.

Sophomore year can be an opportunity for your teen to try a new co-curricular club or spend time developing his/her skills in an area of interest. My younger son had an interest in technology, so he spent his sophomore year learning more about coding through free online courses. This was especially helpful for him since he was not able to take the advanced computer science courses at his high school until his junior and senior year.

Academic exploration is OK, though with limitations. Low sophomore year grades may even be forgiven in a way that junior year grades will not be. However, if your teen's grades were lower than their potential during freshman year, your teen should make every effort to improve his/her grades during sophomore year. When some colleges look at high school transcripts, they look at all years, not just the junior and senior years, and they prefer students whose grades improved during high school.

Recognizing the critical period between the sophomore and junior year, there are summer programs specifically for sophomores, as well as more pre-professional summer programs open to sophomores. For example, Carleton Liberal Arts Experience in Minnesota is focused on African-American students who have completed 10th grade. The CLAE (Carleton Liberal Arts Experience) Program introduces sophomores to liberal arts curriculum at a time when they are most likely to start distinguishing what colleges have to offer.

A recent trend at high schools across the US is sophomore-only programming. If your teen's high school offers such a program, then I applaud their efforts. A high school in Ohio presents a special event for their sophomores focused on self-awareness and personal identity. Having this attention on self-awareness and personal identity positions these 10th graders for a more intentional approach to the college admissions process and discovering their life interests.

Apply A+ Attitudes™ in 10th Grade

Regardless of how involved or not you were during your teen's freshman year of high school, his/her sophomore year will present new areas that you can be engaged in to support his/her educational journey. If you have been on track with the 9th grade roadmap, then you will recognize the routines I previously outlined in the last chapter. However, if you did not use the 9th grade roadmap, then this guide will still be easy to follow.

This sophomore roadmap is meant to help you plan ahead for 10th grade while recognizing these two important developments:

1) Your teen may be in an awkward stage of adolescence.

2) Your teen may start to become more stressed about college.

My hope is that this roadmap is organized in an easy-to-use way so that you can be aware and helpful to your teen, despite all the other demands on your time and attention. For each month, make sure your teen follows through on at least one of the tasks outlined. You should focus intentionally on one task per month because you want to make sure that your teen stays on track and pushes through any "sophomore slump" he/she may experience. I think it's easier to get stuck during 10th grade because students in 9th and 11th ARE getting more attention than the sophomore class.

As you review and take action with this sophomore guide, think of me as partnering with you along your teen's educational journey. Your role throughout this roadmap is to support your teen in taking the actions each month. At no time during this school year should you be taking more actions than your teen!

How to Do 10th Grade with Your Teen Month-by-Month

August

❖ **Together with your teen, set up a 10th grade roadmap for the school year.** There's a sample roadmap at the end of this chapter or you may download a printable version at this link: (theeducationdoctor.com/whattoknow). The printable roadmap, from my website, includes one actionable tip for each month with space for you to add other events or actions throughout the year. When you provide an email address to get the printable roadmap online, you will also receive additional bonus tips throughout your teen's sophomore year to add to your teen's roadmap. To get the most out of your roadmap, please post a printed roadmap where your teen can see it regularly and build solid organizational skills.

❖ **Determine 1-2 goals for your teen's 10th grade year.** Based on reviewing the sophomore roadmap and considering what your teen wants to achieve throughout high school, your teen should be ready to set 1-2 goals for this school year. Examples of goals for 10th grade may be:

- Meet with one teacher two times per month to review class discussions and/or graded assignments.
- Help plan an event for a co-curricular club joined in 9th grade.
- Earn 95%+ score in two core courses for the year.
- Achieve High Honor Roll for a term.
- Spend twenty hours volunteering with a community agency (this should be an agency that your teen cares about).

❖ **Confirm courses.** Review the course schedule for the entire year to ensure that the right classes are included. Any adjustments should be based on the four-year academic plan for your teen (as discussed in "Chapter 4 – Look Forward." If your teen is unable to get his/her top choice course selections, let him/her take the lead in advocating for the courses he/she wants. This will be a good time to show your trust in your teen and send a message him/her that he/she is in charge of his/her learning.

September

❖ **Set up a filing system.** If your teen hasn't already done so, make sure he/she sets up both an online filing system, i.e. Google Drive or Dropbox, to keep online documents and a simple, old-fashioned paper folder system. The online filing system can include folders for each of your teen's courses and folders for college-related topics. A paper system would include manila folders from an office supply store with labelled tabs. Only four or five folders are needed. Your teen can choose from these labels for his/her file folders:

- Sample Essays.
- Scholarships for College
- Honors and Achievements
- Co-curricular Activities
- Basketball or Cross-Country or Football or Lacrosse, etc.
- Interesting Articles
- Testing for College

❖ **Attend at least one social function, if offered.** Most school calendars will include a sporting event or dance early in the fall. This will be an opportunity for your teen to socialize and get reacquainted with students. If there are no school events scheduled for this month, then encourage your teen to spend time outside of school with one friend in his/her class. The goal of these different interactions is that your teen is encouraged to proactively choose good friendships and remove himself/herself from any bad relationships.

❖ **Actively participate in class discussions.** Even if your teen is shy, still encourage him/her to engage in class discussions. Again, this is a way for your teen to take ownership of his/her own learning and start to develop relationships with teachers. Class participation may include asking questions, volunteering for an activity, and/or making comments that add to the discussion. In addition to asking your teen if he/she is speaking up in class, please consider asking 1-2 teachers about your teen's class participation.

October

❖ **Take a practice PSAT.** Taking a practice PSAT (Preliminary Scholastic Aptitude Test) can help your teen get familiar with the SAT. Please keep in mind, however, that the PSAT is NOT used for college admissions so this can be a good way for your teen to learn about the SAT in a less stressful way. I think it's a good idea to take the PSAT in the sophomore year without advance preparation. Although the PSAT may be automatically given to high school juniors, your sophomore may have to request to take the PSAT through his/her school counselor. If your teen is unable to take the PSAT at his/her school as a 10th grader, your teen can go to the College Board website to learn more about the PSAT and download a practice test to take and get a score.

❖ **Set up a professional forwarding email.** Your teen should get an email address that can be used ongoing. This email address can be a variation on his/her given name but certainly NOT hotchick911@domain.com or djquiklove@domain.com. Even if your teen's school pro-vides an email account, I still recommend that he/she has a separate account which can be used continuously since the high school email is only available when your teen is enrolled in high school. One of my students attends a school where he can't even use his school's email account during the summer months.

❖ **Meet with 1-2 teachers outside of class time.** A good habit for your sophomore to continue to develop is proactively meeting with teachers after class. This is yet another way for your 10th grader to own his/her learning experience. Likewise, I encourage students to develop these relationships with their teachers so they learn the importance of self-advocacy and having a network of supporters.

November

❖ **Research scholarships**. There are scholarships for college that your 10th grader may qualify to win. A website your teen can search is unigo.com. Many scholarships may require an essay and there are some scholarships based on books read. Your teen may even consider choosing a book to read based on an available scholarship. For example, there's a scholarship for writing an essay in response to Ayn Rand's *Atlas Shrugged,* and other novels. Your teen can then read this book for the scholarship and complete the next task at the same time. (If your teen finds a scholarship for the next school year, make sure that he/she prints the description of that scholarship and adds it to his/her "Scholarships for College" folder.)

❖ **Read a book**. Your teen should be encouraged to read a book outside of class even during the school year. This month and next month are good times because of the extended holiday breaks. While I understand that your 10th grader may already have a lot of reading to do for his/her classes, encouraging your teen to read for pleasure sends a strong message that reading is a priority. A book to read for pleasure can be any topic of interest. If your teen loves to read anything and everything, encourage him/her to download a list of college classics and choose one to tackle. If your teen struggles to find reading material of interest, encourage him/her to ask a friend, get a recommendation from your local library, or check out teenreads.com.

December

❖ **Complete a personality assessment.** Have your teen take a personality assessment that's written and scored for teens. The results of a personality instrument may provide valuable insights for you and your teen as you investigate various summer programs or pre-college opportunities.

Authors Claire Law and Rosalind P. Marie in *Find the Perfect College for You* encourages the use of Myers-Briggs Type Indicator (MBTI), stating that the MBTI can be useful for understanding how your teen processes information, makes decisions, and relates to the outside world and, thus, can be used to help identify best fit schools. A similar instrument that I use in my own practice is the book, *Do What You Are: Discover the Perfect Career for You Through the Secrets of Personality Type* by Paul D. Tieger and Barbara Barron-Tieger, which is based on MBTI. There are other tools that can be used as well. The key with any instrument like this is that your teen understands what the results mean. Either you can interpret the results with your teen or have your teen's college counselor do so.

❖ **Take a pre-ACT assessment.** Just as some high schools offer the PSAT, some may also have access to pre-ACT exams. The ACT and SAT are different enough that usually students will be more comfortable with one rather than the other. Taking a pre-ACT would give your teen the same opportunity they had with the pre-SAT to learn which test they prefer. The pre-ACT is not used for college admissions purposes so your teen can check out the ACT with little stress. Once the scores are compared, your teen can then decide which test is their best test and focus on that one.

January

❖ **Check grade reports.** Depending on term grades and teacher comments, your teen should use this feedback to decide on next steps for the remainder of the school year. If their grades are strong and match with a strong effort, then the next step is to continue with what they've been doing. If your teen's grades are weak, i.e. below their goal, then the next step is to get help. Help can come from a tutor, additional support from a teacher, extra problems in a review book, or an online course. Your teen should be proactive in figuring out the type of help he/she needs. If it's the case that your teen's grades are a result of laziness or lack of effort, please intervene immediately. The longer you wait to address it, the worse your teen's laziness will become and that will definitely result in more work and stress for YOU! (I see a lot of lazy students in their senior year, and my hunch is that this trait started long before senior year.)

❖ **Start researching summer programs.** The summer after 10th grade is a great time to discover more about a field of study or career interest. Whether or not your sophomore already participated in a summer program after 9th grade, this summer can be a time to learn more about what they already know they are interested in. For example, I mentioned previously that my son had an interest in technology. He pursued that interest further during his summer after 10th grade by attending a computer science camp. If your teen is still undecided about his/her interests, you can use the results of the personality assessments as a way to find a few possible summer programs. Another option may be to find a sophomore-only program that your teen can apply to. If there's a program fee, please find out right away if the summer program offers scholarships so that you can meet their submissions deadline.

❖ **Review PSAT results.** This final step to taking the PSAT is important but often forgotten. Your teen should spend time reviewing the report of their PSAT results and know what his/her score means. If an online account was set up for your teen at the College Board site, then he/she should also know his/her login information. The printed report from your teen's school counselor should be filed in his/her "Testing for College" folder for easy reference later.

February

❖ **Submit summer program applications.** The summer program applications for your sophomore may require teacher recommendations, transcripts, and essays. Whether they are admitted to the programs or not, preparing these applications will be a tremendous experience for your teen. It can also be a reality check for your sophomore if he/she tends to be somewhat arrogant about his/her abilities.

❖ **Search for scholarships.** Whether or not your teen has already researched scholarships back in the fall/winter, checking again may generate a few more scholarships that were overlooked in the prior search. Be sure your teen adds any upcoming deadlines to your family calendar (and on his/her smartphone) so he/she remembers to apply. In addition, remind him/her to track any documents related to the scholarships in his/her online and/or paper filing folder.

March

❖ **Volunteer.** The holidays may present a great time for your teen to volunteer in the local community. Again, my primary rule of thumb is that any volunteering must be done for an organization or cause that your teen cares about. Volunteering just for the sake of college admissions isn't worth the time and effort. When it's time to draft his/her activities resume or write essays, shallow community service will stand out as artificial and insincere.

❖ Monitor Facebook and other social media sites. If your teen has not already started to monitor his/her social media accounts, now is a good time for your teen to learn how to self-monitor. Actively self-monitoring means that your teen should clean-up his/her posts. If there is any negative or profane language in his/her posts, he/she should clean them up or remove them immediately. This also includes posts on his/her page from friends and family members. Likewise, I encourage YOU to be connected to your teen on social media accounts where possible and also monitor what your teen is doing online if you have not already been doing so. Too many parents take a hands-off approach to social media and I find that disappointing. Given the public and viral nature of social media, you can never be too careful about the negative impact of an inappropriate social media post nor its longevity.

April

❖ **Attend a college fair**. While there is no need to officially visit colleges during sophomore year, a local college fair is appropriate. Local college fairs are usually announced in the newspaper or through your high school college counseling office. Also, you may check out the website for the National Association for College Admission Counseling at nacacnet.org which posts national college fairs. At the end of this chapter, you will find a handy guide entitled, "How to Make the Most of a College Fair," followed by a checklist to use during the fair.

❖ **Compare ACT and SAT test results.** Now that your teen has results from both PSAT and pre-ACT, he/she can use an online ACT-SAT comparison table to determine which test is best. I recommend that your teen takes either the ACT or SAT, but not both. It's a waste of time and money to take both tests because colleges nowadays will accept either test. (And if your teen doesn't want to take any standardized tests, there are about 1000 colleges in the US that do not require the ACT or SAT.) Since all colleges will accept either test, then your teen has the leverage to focus on what works best for him/her.

❖ **Stay on track with study plans for AP exam.** If your teen takes an Advanced Placement course in his/her sophomore year, then April is a great time to study well for the AP exams in May. Additionally, your teen should consider registering for the corresponding SAT Subject Test. (See 11th grade monthly roadmap in next chapter for more details on AP and SAT Subject Tests.)

May

❖ **Advanced Placement tests.** Your teen will take any AP exams during the first two weeks of May. (See the sample schedule in the 11th grade monthly roadmap in next chapter or you may go to my website (theeducationdoctor.com) and search for "AP test dates" to find the upcoming schedule for your teen.)

❖ **Determine your teen's testing plan for his/her junior year.** Based on which test your teen wants to take in his/ her junior year, visit the actstudent.org or collegeboard.org to view his/her testing calendars for the next school year. I would recommend that your teen plans to take the same test twice during 11th grade (next school year). Of course, it would be great if your teen scored at his/her highest potential on the first time, but most teens do not. Planning for a second test date leaves the teen more flexibility to retake for a higher score without having to retake again in his/her senior year.

❖ **Finalize your teen's summer calendar.** After your teen has heard back from all summer program applications, you can plan for the summer. Having one formal summer program in place will help with planning the other weeks of the summer which should include time to relax, enjoy time with friends, read, and just be himself/herself.

June

❖ **Take SAT Subject test(s).** These tests should only be taken if your teen took an AP course during 10th grade. If not, please don't worry that your teen is "missing out"... He/she is still on track for college admissions success!

❖ **Set a summer reading plan.** As I discussed in "Chapter 2 Prepare Before High School," reading for pleasure is key to getting in and getting money for college. If your teen is a reluctant reader, the local library is a great resource for helping your teen find books to read this summer and even joining a summer reading challenge. I highly recommend participation in a summer reading challenge for your 10th grader because it will make reading more fun and offer a place for your teen to make friends with other readers... another opportunity for your teen to make wise friendship choices as discussed in "September" of this 10th grade roadmap.

❖ **Update activities resume.** Now that the school year has come to a close, it's a great idea for your teen to update his/her activities resume for 10th grade while it's still fresh in mind. Updating the activities resume now will help with determining summer goals and be a reality check on what to do or not do in 11th grade.

July
❖ Enjoy summer activities and keep on reading!

Bonus

COMPASS

Sophomore Monthly Roadmap

In addition to this Roadmap to Get In Get Money™ for college, you will receive weekly update emails with additional real-time tips to add to this checklist. I would love to partner with you to achieve your teen's educational vision. Please contact me today - drpamela@theeducationdoctor.com

August
- [ ] Set academic and social goals
- [ ] _____

September
- [ ] Update activities resume
- [ ] _____

October
- [ ] Join 1-2 clubs at school
- [ ] _____

November
- [ ] Participate in class discussions
- [ ] _____

December
- [ ] Read a book during winter break
- [ ] _____

January
- [ ] Meet with teacher(s) to overview 2nd semester objectives
- [ ] _____

February
- [ ] Apply to summer programs
- [ ] _____

March
- [ ] Attend college fair with your College Fair ReadiGuide™
- [ ] _____

April
- [ ] Determine junior year courses
- [ ] _____

May
- [ ] Set summer reading plan and calendar
- [ ] _____

June: **This is your summer to "*Discover*"... Enjoy!**

Pamela Ellis, The Education Doctor®, has helped thousands of teens attend a college that feels like home. She brings 25 years of experience in education to assist with college selection, admissions, financial aid, and freshman transition success. Dr. Pamela holds a PhD from Stanford and MBA from Dartmouth. For tips and tools to help your college-bound teen, visit compasscollegeadvisory.com.

Copyright @2017 by Compass Education Strategies, LLC. All Rights Reserved. The Education Doctor is a USPTO registered trademark.

Copy and post this checklist to keep track of expectations and actions to navigate 10th grade year.

Bonus: How to Make the Most of a College Fair

College fairs are a great way to initially learn about those colleges that may be a good fit for your teen. College-bound teens may want to attend a college fair in their sophomore or junior year. Although the college fair does not replace a campus visit, it can be a great, low-cost way to create a short list of colleges to visit.

Given the large number of colleges represented at these fairs, you and your teen may feel overwhelmed by where to start. Your teen should take the lead with preparing for the college fair beforehand and certainly meeting with college representatives during the fair. Your role, as the parent/guardian, is to support your teen's attendance at the fair but avoid doing the advance preparation for your teen and limiting your conversations with college representatives during the fair.

What to do several days before the visit:

1) Determine which college representatives to meet.

2) Prepare questions to ask college representatives at the fair. (See the "College Fair Comparison Checklist" following for suggestions).

3) Print pre-printed labels with your contact information.

What to do during the college fair:

1) Use the "College Fair Comparison Checklist" (following) to keep track of each college.

2) Make sure you get a business card from college representatives in case you want to email or call later.

3) Visit with a college representative that's not busy and *not* on your list. Learning about this new contact will help you learn about other colleges and broaden your perspective on them.

What to do after the college fair:

Send an email, or even better, handwritten notes, to thank the college representatives for their time at the college fair.

Bonus: College Fair Comparison Checklist

College Fair Checklist

How to make the most of College Fairs

College fairs are a great way to find those colleges that are a good fit for teens. College-bound teens may want to attend a college fair in their sophomore or junior year. Keep in mind that it does not replace a campus visit, but can be a great, low cost way to determine which colleges to visit.

Given the large number of colleges represented at these fairs, parents and teens can feel overwhelmed by where to start.

Days before the visit:

1. Determine which college representatives you want to meet

2. Prepare questions (see next page for suggestions) to ask college representatives at the fair

3. Print pre-printed labels with your contact information.

During the college fair:

4. Use comparison checklist (see next page) to keep track of each college

5. Make sure you get a business card from college representatives in case you want to email or call later.

6. Visit with a college representative that's not busy and <u>not</u> on your list. Learning about this new contact will inform your perspective on other colleges.

Pamela Ellis, The Education Doctor®, has helped thousands of teens attend a college that feels like home. She brings 25 years of experience in education to assist with college selection, admissions, financial aid, and freshman transition success. Dr. Pamela holds a PhD from Stanford and MBA from Dartmouth. For tips and tools to help your college-bound teen, visit compasscollegeadvisory.com.

Bonus: Tips and Resources for Sophomores

Books

This book, *How to Become a Straight-A Student* by Cal Newport, has many suggestions that your teen can apply immediately.

Campus Visit Tips for Sophomores

The most common question I get from parents with sophomores is, "Which college campuses should we visit?" The short answer is, "It depends." I don't have a more specific answer because most sophomores are still figuring out high school, so researching colleges seems to add too much unnecessary stress. If your family already has plans to travel to an area, then I recommend visiting a mix of colleges in that local area. The colleges can vary by size of student body, urban vs. rural setting, religious affiliation, or selectivity. What I see most often is that parents tend to take their teens to the most selective, name-brand colleges too early, which sends a message that those colleges are the only ones worth visiting.

Aside from a formal campus visit, your teen can visit the college campus in an informal way such as to go to a college basketball game, watch a theatrical performance, or simply walk around a college campus and visit the library or dining hall. These casual types of visits can help your teen learn about the life of a college student.

For any type of visit, here are a few suggestions for your teen to make the most of your time on the college campus:

- Read about the campus before your visit to get a sense for what is said about campus life and which places to visit.

- Don't just talk to tour guides, ask a few questions of random students about their college experience.

- Read the bulletin board, kiosks, and student newspaper.
- Remember to record impressions and observations in real time (or soon afterwards) so you don't forget the details about your visit.

Each college has its own personality and culture. Encourage your teen to keep an open mind so that his/her options stay open through the senior year. These early impressions are not the end-all-be-all for his/her college decision two years from now.

Summer Programs
- Carleton Liberal Arts Experience - This is a one-week summer program that introduces the strengths of a liberal arts education through an array of courses in science, art, social sciences, and technology.
- Economics for Leaders *(EFL)* - This program gives students the skills to be more effective leaders and to teach them how to apply economic analysis when considering public policy choices.

The Education Doctor® Podcasts
These podcast episodes are relevant for sophomore year:
- "What Parents Must Know about Testing for College Admissions"
- "How to Help Your Teen Write Better"
- "When is it Too Soon for a Campus Visit"

You can download at theeducationdoctor.com/whattoknow

Useful websites
- actstudent.org - see ACT testing dates, register to take test in 11th grade (next school year) and get scores.

- collegeboard.org - see SAT testing dates, register to take the official test in 11th grade (next school year) and get scores; see AP schedule and get scores (usually available in early July)
- fairtest.org - lists colleges that are "test optional," i.e., they do not require SAT or ACT for admissions.

Chapter 7
Junior Year (Connect)

One comment that I hear most frequently from my students in 11th grade is "It's harder!" Junior year of high school may indeed feel "harder" because students are usually taking an Advanced Placement course for the first time. Since most high schools will reserve the AP and Honors courses for juniors and seniors, I often see juniors who are taking too many AP/Honors courses in the same year. I applaud those schools that limit the number of AP courses a student can take in one school year.

There's already increased attention on the college admissions process in the junior year. An intense academic workload adds to the stress and anxiety already surrounding college admissions because students may overload on AP/Honors courses to "look good for colleges." One of my students even took only AP courses in junior and senior year to maintain his class ranking. Yikes!

If your teen is attending a college prep high school, then the junior year is certainly when he/she will feel more stressed about college admissions. Most high schools start the college admissions process in the junior year, usually spring. My hope is that because *you* decided to read this book, you started the college admissions process long before spring of junior year. When a teen starts the college admissions process in spring of junior year, he/she may have limited control over his/her college list and potentially fewer options for getting in and getting money.

To illustrate the importance of starting earlier than junior year, I will share a brief case study:

> **Case in point:** "Sally" is a teen who aspired to study computer science in college. Her parents had not attended college, but valued higher education and envisioned that Sally would attend college after high school. Sally attended a "good" public high school, so her parents assumed that her high school counselor was guiding her towards college. Sally started her college admissions process by signing up for her first SAT in the fall of senior year. With taking the SAT for the first time in the senior year, she won't get her test scores in time to know how competitive her application will compare to peers who apply to the same colleges as she does. When Sally started researching colleges, she realized that a few colleges that she liked recommended that applicants submit a Math II Subject Test. She was taking Precalculus in her senior year so there was no way that she could be prepared to take a Math II Subject Test before the January application deadline. Just this brief synopsis of Sally's story shows how a late start can limit a teen's chances of getting in and getting money for college.

Ease Up in Junior Year

Your Junior may begin to feel this college "pressure" in specific ways like:

- **Being invited by a college to attend an on-campus "junior experience program"** where your teen can learn about that college through tours and/or overnight stay.

- **Receiving an increasing amount of mail from colleges,** especially after taking the ACT or SAT.

Although your teen may be a great student, colleges are wooing thousands of other students. So, please help your teen keep these mailings in perspective and understand that these marketing materials do not imply that your teen will be admitted to the colleges.

- **Overhearing conversations or talking with peers about college admissions.** Talk about college admissions among teens often stems from conversations at home from parents. This is a sore spot for me with my children because I'm a college admissions professional. It would be so easy for me to talk about colleges all the time, but I am very cautious about limiting how much I talk about their own college paths so that they own it for themselves.

- **Feeling stress and/or anxious about testing.** Testing during the junior year can allow students to discover how competitive their scores are for the colleges they target. At the same time, testing in a student's junior year can raise even more stress for these students at the same time that they are challenged with a heavier workload. I urge parents to not overburden their teen with "test stress." Too much stress about test prep, testing, and scores is misplaced and takes away from true learning. If your teen has test anxiety and/or scores "low" on these standardized tests, then there are about a thousand colleges that are test-optional, i.e., they do not require a test score!

- **Having a more accelerated college admissions process if your teen is a recruited athlete.** Recruited athletes may have to take SAT or ACT even in fall of their junior year to submit scores to colleges. A provisional acceptance may be given to a recruited athlete in the spring of junior year.

As your junior starts to feel the pressure of college, I would advise you to continue to let your junior lead the process. You can be aware of what's expected of your teen during this critical year, however, it's even more important that you "ease back" and let him/her earnestly own the process.

Apply A+ Attitudes™ in 11th grade

Your junior must take ownership of the college admission process now if he/she hasn't already done so. Ownership means that your teen should be responsible and accountable for taking actions such as:

- Researching colleges.
- Communicating with colleges, including RSVP'ing for campus visits.
- Registering for his/her SAT or ACT test dates.
- Requesting recommendations from teachers.

Yes, I have known parents who are doing all these tasks for their teens. The interactions with the school counselor, teachers, and college representatives must be done by your teen. If you communicate on his/her behalf, especially to the colleges, it will weaken his/her admissions chances. Teens who are accustomed to their parents doing everything for them have the least satisfaction in their college choices and a more difficult adjustment to adulthood.

A key focus of junior year for your teen should be nurturing teacher relationships. While it's still important for your teen to actively participate in the school community and put forth his/her best effort in academic courses, building a positive relationship with teachers can't be overlooked.

Junior year teachers play a critical role in the application process in that they will likely write teacher recommendations for your teens. The teacher recommendations must come from a teacher in math, language arts, social studies, science, or foreign language. (In the case of "Sally" whom I discussed previously, she only had a strong relationship with her band teacher and didn't feel comfortable asking any core teacher for a recommendation. Unless Sally will be a music major and a member of the college marching band, then most colleges will still require a recommendation from a core academic subject teacher.) Key qualities of recommending teachers should be that they:

- Know the student well.
- Write well.

It doesn't matter if the student earned an "A" in the course; what matters is that the student was challenged and worked hard in that teacher's course. Students will often ask me "How can I know if a teacher is a good writer?" My response is that they ask other seniors about their experiences with a recommending teacher. Also, students may see examples of a teacher's writing style from their own semester grade reports or comments from exams. I learned about the writing quality of my son's teachers from his semester grade reports since he attended a school where teachers wrote extensively about his classroom performance each term. It was clear from those grade reports which teachers could write with greater clarity to best support his college applications.

This junior roadmap will keep you aware of what's happening in the college admissions process. If you are just starting the college admissions process, I urge you to read through the roadmaps for 9th and 10th grades to make sure that your teen is best prepared to take full advantage of this process during junior year. Even if your teen is delayed in starting the process, the process will not wait for them and your teen will have a lot of catch-up to do.

For each month of the junior year roadmap, make sure your teen follows through on each task outlined. Junior year is not the time for them to slack off in any way, and it's especially not appropriate for you to do the tasks for your teen. Your role throughout this roadmap is to support your teen in taking the actions each month.

As you review and take action with this junior guide, think of me as partnering and coaching you along your teen's educational journey. I want to impress upon you the urgency of junior year as I see too many teens who miss out on getting into a college of their choice and getting money for college because they waited too late. If parents know to "light a fire" under their teen and the steps to take and then take them, more college dreams with less debt can be realized.

How to Do 11th Grade with Your Teen Month-by-Month

August

❖ **Together with your teen, set up an 11th grade road-map for the school year.** There's a sample roadmap at the end of this chapter or you may download a printable version at this link: (theeducationdoctor.com/whattoknow). The printable roadmap, from my website, includes one actionable tip for each month with space for you to add other events or actions throughout the year. When you provide an email address to get the printable roadmap online, you will also receive additional bonus tips through-out your teen's junior year to add to his/her roadmap. To get the most out of your roadmap, please post a printed roadmap where your teen can see it regularly and build solid organizational skills.

❖ **Determine 1-2 goals for your teen's 11th grade year.** Based on reviewing the junior roadmap and considering what your teen wants to achieve for the remaining years of high school, your teen should be ready to set 1-2 goals for this school year. Examples of goals for 11th grade may be:

- Meet with one teacher two times per month to review class discussion and/or graded assignments.

- Get elected or selected for a leadership role in one of the clubs joined in 9th grade.

- Earn 95%+ score in three core courses for the year.

- Spend fifteen hours volunteering with the community agency (be sure that it's an agency/cause that your teen cares about).

- Visit five new college campuses that could be a fit.

❖ **Confirm courses.** Review the course schedule for the entire year to ensure that the right classes are included. Any adjustments should be based on the four-year academic plan for your teen (as discussed in "Chapter 4 – Look Forward"). If your teen is unable to get his/her top choice course selections, let your teen take the lead on determining whether to stick with the courses or petition to switch his/her schedule.

❖ **Confirm your teen's plan for junior year testing.** The best test prep tutors usually fill their student rosters quickly so your teen should contact them well ahead of his/her first scheduled test date. Likewise, it's important for your teen to meet with his/her tutor beforehand to make sure he/she feels comfortable working with that tutor. If your teen preps with a tutor that he/she doesn't feel comfortable with, then it's not only a big waste of time and money but may also jeopardize your teen's scores. (The rates for test prep tutors can vary from $25/hour to well over $150/hour... so take care with this decision by interviewing and checking references.)

September

❖ **Run for a leadership role.** If your teen has been actively participating in a club for the past two years, encourage him/her to run for a leadership role. There may also be class-wide leadership opportunities like junior class officers or student council representatives. The experience of running for a leadership role as a junior can be a great learning experience and preparation for your teen's senior year.

❖ **Actively participate in class discussions.** Even if your teen is shy, encourage him/her to engage in class discussion. Again, this is a way for your teen to take ownership of his/her own learning and nurture these important relationships with junior-year teachers. Class participation may include asking questions, volunteering for an activity, and/or making comments that add to the discussion.

October

❖ **Take PSAT.** Before taking this test, it is worth asking "What is the PSAT?" and "Why should my teen take it?" The Preliminary Scholastic Aptitude Test results are used for students to be recognized and perhaps qualify for National Merit Scholarships. This test is typically mandatory for most high school juniors in the US. Other than National Merit scholarship considerations, the PSAT results have limited use. Whether your teen studies for it though is another question. I generally do not recommend that students study for the PSAT if they *do not* already have a score in the 95+ percentile from a prior year. Prioritizing course grades in the junior year is far more important than prepping for a PSAT that is not part of the scores submitted for college admissions. (Any test prep during 11th grade is best spent on either your teen's scheduled ACT dates or SAT dates.)

❖ **Start strong with reading coursework, taking notes systematically, and reviewing notes after class.** Your teen's grades should continue to be strong–or get even better–as the coursework may become more difficult in the junior year. A drop in grades from sophomore to junior year may signal to college admissions officers that the student is not willing or able to take on the rigors of a college curriculum.

November

❖ **Start researching colleges.** This should be more than just looking at images on college websites. I recommend that the initial list of colleges your teen researches represents a cross-section by selectivity, size, major emphasis, location, and geography. Whether your teen researches 3-4 colleges that are already familiar to him/her or colleges that are totally new, your teen should research specific information about each college such as:

- Key admissions statistics, like admissions rate, enrollment rate, and percentage of freshmen from out of state.
- Academic–which courses are required for major interests, a faculty member of interest, high school courses required for major interests.
- Social statistics–percentage of freshmen in undergraduate housing, what the housing policy is, specific clubs of interest, traditions to learn more about.
- Financial–the percentage of students receiving financial aid, and/or merit scholarships that may be a match.

A helpful resource for your teen's research may include the *Fiske Guide to Colleges* because its descriptions are very detailed and often include a summary of other comparable colleges that your teen may also want to consider. The end of this chapter includes a "College Research Checklist" that can be used to research each college consistently and thoroughly.

December

❖ **Schedule any weekend open house events for juniors at local and/or regional campuses of interest.** These visits should be limited to colleges that your teen researched previously. Junior year is too important and too busy to waste time visiting colleges for the sake of visiting! It's a waste of time and money for your teen to visit colleges that he/she has not already taken the time to learn more about so that his/her visit is intentional and productive.

❖ **Research summer programs.** Many of the summer programs offered after junior year are competitive and may have application deadlines in January or February. To ensure that your teen meets the deadline, encourage him/her to start looking for potential formal programs to apply to for next summer. The bonus section of this chapter includes a few summer programs that may raise your teen's curiosity about available opportunities. These competitive applications typically require recommendations and essays that your teen should leave plenty of time to prepare in advance of the deadline.

❖ **Confirm SAT/ACT study plan.** Whether your teen is studying on his/her own or working with a tutor, please encourage your teen to have an actionable plan in place for how he/she will prepare for either the ACT or SAT. (The focus should be on one or the other test... not both.)

January

❖ **Submit summer program applications.** The summer program applications for your junior will likely be competitive programs that will require teacher recommendations, transcripts, test scores, and essays. Even when my junior clients will not be able to attend a summer program, I still encourage them to apply to one selective program so they can get the experience of having a junior year teacher write a recommendation, practice writing essays, and see how their application compares with other juniors. If your teen is not admitted to a summer program, he/she may be able to get some feedback as to why the college made this decision. One of my students learned that one of the reasons her application was denied was that her teacher did not submit the teacher recommendation. While her family was very upset at her teacher, I thought it was a valuable lesson to learn which teacher(s) to ask for a recommendation and which teachers NOT to ask. The college admissions process is not forgiving when a teacher fails to submit the needed recommendation. Furthermore, it is always a good idea to check that a teacher has submitted a recommendation. If the teacher has not, then confirm that he/she can still do it or find another reliable recommender.

- ❖ **Check grade reports.** Depending on term grades and teacher comments, your teen should use this feedback to decide on next steps for the remainder of the school year. If your teen's grades are strong and match with a strong effort, then the next step is to continue with what he/she has already been doing. If your teen's grades are weak, i.e., below his/her goal, then the next step is to get immediate help from the subject teacher, an outside tutor, or an online course. Your teen should be proactive in figuring out the type of help that will make a difference in his/her improving his/her grade. If your teen is lazy and not putting forth the effort, please intervene right away. The longer you wait to address this issue, the worse it will get. Likewise, your teen's laziness will put more pressure on you to do the college admissions process for him/her, which will ultimately hurt your teen's chances of getting into and getting money for college.

February

❖ **Plan spring campus visits.** An ideal time for your junior to visit college campuses will be during spring break. During that time, classes may be in session at the various college campuses and your junior may be able to meet an admissions representative. Spring break is a popular time for many families to visit colleges so your teen should RSVP about six weeks before so that you and your teen can be scheduled for both an information session and a campus tour. A sample campus visit itinerary at the end of this chapter shows the advance planning necessary to make the most of your teen's campus visits.

❖ **Search for scholarships.** There are several scholarships available only to seniors. This month is a great time for your teen to search for those upcoming scholarships, determine their qualifications, and put the deadlines on the calendar. There will be so many deadlines to remember once your teen applies to college so keeping all deadlines on one calendar will help keep everyone on track. In addition, remind your teen to track any documents related to the scholarships in his/her online and paper filing folder. (Again, because of the busy-ness of the junior and senior years, it will be a good practice to keep a duplicate file of what's online and printed so no deadline is missed.)

March

❖ **Visit 3-5 colleges during spring break.** Junior year campus visits are very important for college applications, especially essays. I recommend that visits are limited to 1-2 campuses a day and that each visit includes an infor-mation session and campus tour. Your teen should have RSVP's for these visits so that each college has a record of his/her visit. For some colleges, this "demonstrated interest" can help your teen with both admissions and scholarships. One last tip for your campus visit... please remind your teen that when he/she sets foot on the college campus, he/she is being "interviewed." Your teen should leave moodiness, a bad attitude, talking back, and acting out, i.e. clowning, at home. Likewise, if your teen has not researched the college and/or is not interested in visiting, save your time and money. Junior year is too important and busy for you to take your teen to a college campus because YOU want your teen to apply there. At the end of this chapter, you will find a printable campus visit checklist to use for each college.

❖ **Register for spring test retake.** Now that your teen has learned his/her test scores for the SAT or ACT, set a second test for the spring of junior year if your teen wants to raise his/her score. I suggest that any test retakes are done in the spring of junior year because senior year will already be busy enough without the stress of retaking an ACT or SAT. Your teen should be certain to plan ahead to prepare for the retake. If your teen does not have the time to prepare, then a retake should not be scheduled. It's a waste of time and money to "wing" an ACT or SAT, especially at this critical time in the college admissions process.

April

❖ **Attend a college fair.** Colleges that your teen is interested in learning more about that he/she has not visited would be worth meeting at a local college fair. The emphasis is on "local" because I do not want to suggest that you drive great distances at an inconvenience, just for the sake of attending a college fair. Sometimes, the college tables at a fair may be represented with an alum who is less connected with current campus life or the table is only filled with brochures which you can have mailed to your home. Another type of college fair that your junior may be "invited" to attend is a college "roadshow" which is a group of colleges that present an off-campus information session for families who may be unable to travel to their campuses. I will put it bluntly by saying that I'm not a big fan of these roadshows. Too often, the roadshows are only presented by the most selective, brand-name colleges; they are often over-subscribed with stressed-out teens who are only interested in applying because of the brand-name. And I must admit that when I have attended these "roadshows," stressed-out parents have taken over the sessions with their questions and jockeying for attention. I've noticed that the closer teens get to application season, the more frustrated parents become due to competition and anxiety from other parents. (We set the example for our teens, right?)

May

❖ **Advanced Placement Tests.** If your teen has taken an AP course this year, then he/she will likely take any AP exams during the first two weeks of May. (Some high schools mandate that your teen take the AP test(s) if he/she is enrolled in the course(s).) Here's a sample schedule of AP exams:

Sample AP Test Schedule		
Week 1	**Mornings:**	**Afternoons:**
Monday	Chemistry	Psychology
	Environmental Science	
Tuesday	Computer Science A	Art History
	Spanish Language and Culture	Physics 1: Algebra-Based
Wednesday	English Literature and Composition	Japanese Language and Culture
		Physics 2: Algebra-Based
Thursday	United States Government and Politics	Chinese Language and Culture Seminar
Friday	German Language and Culture	Computer Science Principles
	United States History	

You may check my website (theeducationdoctor.com) and search for "AP test dates" to find the current schedule for your teen.

❖ **Request teacher recommendations for college applications.** Your teen must obtain a recommendation from a teacher in a core academic subject:

- English
- Science
- Math
- Social Studies
- Foreign language

Your teen should request a recommendation from two teachers. Having two recommenders can be helpful for cutting the workload in half so that no one teacher is overburdened with your teen's recommendation letters. Likewise, there may be a college on your teen's list that requires two recommenders. The request should be done by your teen, providing the teacher with an updated activities resume and sharing the reason that particular colleges (3-4) are on his/her short list. The idea is that your teen should make it as easy as possible for the teacher to write a strong recommendation on his/her behalf. Your teen will be in a better position to get a strong, thoughtful, well-written recommendation if he/she requests it before summer (at the end of the junior year).

June

❖ **Take SAT Subject test(s).** These tests should only be taken if your teen took an AP course during his/her junior year. However, if your teen takes Pre-Calculus and has interest in a STEM major, then I would recommend your teen considers taking the Math II SAT Subject test.

❖ **Set a summer reading plan.** As I discussed in "Chapter 2– Prepare Before High School," reading for pleasure is key to getting in and getting money for college. If your teen is a reluctant reader, the local library is a great resource for helping your teen find books to read this summer and even joining a summer reading challenge. I highly recommend participation in a summer reading challenge for your junior to make sure that they are well-prepared to write about these books in their college application essays.

❖ **Update activities resume.** Now that the school year has come to a close, it's a great idea for your teen to update his/her activities resume while it's still fresh in mind. Updating the activities resume now will help with determining summer goals and be a reality check on what to do or not do in 12th grade.

July
❖ Enjoy summer activities and keep on reading!

Bonus

Junior Monthly Roadmap

In addition to this Roadmap to Get In Get Money™ for college, you will receive weekly update emails with additional real-time tips to add to this checklist. I would love to partner with you to achieve your teen's educational vision. Please contact me today - drpamela@theeducationdoctor.com

August
- ☐ Set academic and social goals for junior year
- ☐ _____

September
- ☐ Review activities resume to assist with goal-setting
- ☐ _____

October
- ☐ Take PSAT
- ☐ _____

November
- ☐ Determine testing plan for junior year
- ☐ _____

December
- ☐ Read a book during winter break
- ☐ _____

January
- ☐ Apply to summer program(s)
- ☐ _____

February
- ☐ Continue researching colleges
- ☐ _____

March
- ☐ Visit 3+ college campuses that match your BestFit Profile™
- ☐ _____

April
- ☐ Determine senior year courses
- ☐ _____

May
- ☐ Register for any required SAT 2(s)
- ☐ _____

June: **This is your summer to "Connect"... Enjoy!**

Pamela Ellis, The Education Doctor®, has helped thousands of teens attend a college that feels like home. She brings 25 years of experience in education to assist with college selection, admissions, financial aid, and freshman transition success. Dr. Pamela holds a PhD from Stanford and MBA from Dartmouth. For tips and tools to help your college-bound teen, visit compasscollegeadvisory.com.

Copy and post this checklist to keep track of expectations and actions to navigate 11th grade year.

Bonus: College Research Checklist

Plan to spend about 30-60 minutes reviewing information about each prospective college. This guide will help you research each college consistently so that it's easier to keep track of why a particular college is the best fit for you!

	College/University 1	College/University 2
Admissions rate		
Enrollment rate		
4-year graduation rate		
Percentage of freshmen from out of state		
Required courses in college for major interests		
Faculty member doing interesting research		
High school courses that I must complete for major in college		
Percentage of freshmen in undergraduate housing		
Housing policy		
Specific clubs I would want to join		
Traditions that appeal to me		
Percentage of students receiving financial aid		
Potential merit scholarships		
Career placement record		
% of undergrads who go to grad school		

Bonus: Campus Visit Guide

Campus Visit Guide

This handy guide will be your best resource for writing an application essay that helps you Get in and Get money™ for college! Remember to write your thoughts soon after your visit so that your campus visits don't blur together.

Campus: _____ Location: _____
Admissions contact: _____
Email: _____
Visit date: _____ Tour time: _____ am/pm
Reason for visit: _____
First impressions: _____

ON-CAMPUS IMPRESSIONS: (Rate each category with 5 as best)

	1	2	3	4	5
Classrooms	☐	☐	☐	☐	☐
Access to professors	☐	☐	☐	☐	☐
Research options	☐	☐	☐	☐	☐
Academic support	☐	☐	☐	☐	☐
Study abroad options	☐	☐	☐	☐	☐
Library	☐	☐	☐	☐	☐
Freshman housing	☐	☐	☐	☐	☐
Food/dining	☐	☐	☐	☐	☐
Student center	☐	☐	☐	☐	☐
Athletics	☐	☐	☐	☐	☐
Fitness Center	☐	☐	☐	☐	☐
Political climate	☐	☐	☐	☐	☐
Student clubs of interest	☐	☐	☐	☐	☐
Career resources	☐	☐	☐	☐	☐
Campus security	☐	☐	☐	☐	☐
Overall campus "feel"	☐	☐	☐	☐	☐

Type of student this college/university seeks _____

Level of academic challenge? _____ Too easy (Watch out, this is a Red Flag) _____ Just right _____ Prefer more

Potential major(s) at this college/university _____

OFF-CAMPUS IMPRESSIONS: (Rate each category with 5 as best)

	1	2	3	4	5
Closest city/town	☐	☐	☐	☐	☐
Nearby restaurants	☐	☐	☐	☐	☐
Weekend activities	☐	☐	☐	☐	☐
Local nightlife	☐	☐	☐	☐	☐
Outdoor activities	☐	☐	☐	☐	☐
Public transportation	☐	☐	☐	☐	☐

What stood out as a fit? _____

Interview at this campus? _____ Yes _____ No _____ Not avail
If Yes, scheduled date: _____

Apply? _____ Yes _____ No _____ Not sure
If Yes, which deadline: _____ EA _____ ED _____ Regular

Pamela Ellis, The Education Doctor®, has helped thousands of teens attend a college that feels like home. She brings 25 years of experience in education to assist with college selection, admissions, financial aid, and freshman transition success. Dr. Pamela holds a PhD from Stanford and MBA from Dartmouth. For more tips and tools for college-bound teens, visit compasscollegeadvisory.com.

Bonus: How to Make the Most of the Campus Visit

1) Print your Campus Visit Checklist(s) the night before each visit.

2) Get a good night's rest the night before; visits can be draining.

3) Prepare 1-2 questions that you'd like to ask during the visit. Feel free to use the same 1-2 questions for each visit as a way to compare later.

4) Arrive on campus about fifteen minutes earlier than your appointed time to find parking and check-in for visit

5) Take notes using your Campus Visit Checklist.

6) Say "hello" to the admissions officer that represents your city. If the admissions officer is not available, please get his/her business card to send a follow-up email.

7) Talk to students who are NOT tour guides to learn different perspectives.

8) If there's time before or afterwards, drive/walk around the local neighborhood to get a sense for its appeal and things to do.

Bonus: Sample Campus Visit Itinerary

This mock itinerary shows the necessary advance preparation to make the most of your teen's college campus visit.

Monday, March 31 - Flight Itinerary

- Delta Airlines #2222

  Departs Minneapolis at 7 a.m., arrives Charlotte at 3 p.m.

- Rental car agency–Avis, Confirmation #123X456392
- Hotel - Name, address, and phone number

Tuesday, April 1

- 7:00 a.m.–Depart Charlotte.

  Drive from Charlotte to Greenville - estimated drive time 1 hour and 40 minutes

- 9:00 a.m.–Furman University

    300 Poinsett Hwy.
    Greenville, SC 29613
    (864) 294-2018

- Information session and campus tour—approximately 2-1/2 hours. Parking nearby.
- 11:30 a.m.–Lunch with current students

  Drive from Greenville to Williamsburg, VA—6-1/2 hours

- Local hotel near Williamsburg, VA - Name and phone number

Wednesday, April 2

- 8:30 a.m. - Depart hotel to drive to campus
- 9:00 a.m. College of William and Mary

    116 Jamestown Rd.
    Williamsburg, VA

- Information session and campus tour—approximately 2-1/2 hours. Parking lot available. However, if no parking space, go to Colonial Williamsburg **P6 parking lot.** After bearing right around the corner, turn left onto Route 5 East/Francis Street by Berret's Seafood Restaurant. The P6 parking lot is located immediately to right. There is a **$1 per hour fee**, and the campus visitor parking permit is not honored.

Drive from Williamsburg to Charlottesville, VA–2 hours

- 2:00 pm - University of Virginia

    Newcomb Hall Theater

Parking:

    400 Emmet Street South
    Charlottesville, VA 22904

From the top floor of the Garage (the University Bookstore level), walk across the plaza and enter through the Newcomb Hall portico. As you enter through two sets of doors, turn left and go down the stairs. The entrance to the Theater will be at the end of the lobby on the left-hand side.

Drive from Charlottesville to Lynchburg, VA to meet Robinson family for dinner—1 hour

    Arthur and Lynette Robinson
    123 Madison Street - Lynchburg, VA
    (804) 489-4608

Bonus: Tips and Resources for Juniors

Books

- *Colleges That Change Lives: 40 Schools That Will Change the Way You Think About Colleges* by Loren Pope (website: ctcl.org). This book describes forty selected colleges that take a personalized approach to college admissions and the collegiate experience. I have noticed that these colleges focus more on student potential rather than test scores. Likewise, the collegiate experience is more about community than competition.

- *Fiske Guide* by Ted Fiske has detailed descriptive summaries of colleges throughout the US. A handy feature of this book is a list of "Overlap Colleges." Your teen can use the list of overlap colleges to find other colleges that may also be a match for your teen's interests and needs including colleges that are hidden gems that your teen may not have known about beforehand.

- *There Is Life After College* by Jeffrey J. Selingo. This book is insightful and bound to make you and your teen rethink your teen's college list.

Summer programs for rising seniors only

- Air Force Academy–summer seminar to experience cadet life first-hand.

- MITES at Massachusetts Institute of Technology–intensive six-week residential program for students interested in pursuing STEM

- University of Notre Dame Summer Leadership–discussion-focused seminars exploring topics that affect the global community

The Education Doctor® Podcasts

These podcast episodes are relevant for junior year:

- "SAT Subject Tests: What Parents Must Know"
- "Top 5 Tips for a Stress-Free Campus Visit"
- "5 College Admissions Deadlines Every Parent Must Understand"

You can download at theeducationdoctor.com/whattoknow

Useful Websites for Test Prep

- ineedapencil.ck12.org–free SAT help.
- Khanacademy.org–free SAT help.
- Kranse.com–online SAT prep course that helped my son and other students raise their test scores. If your teen is interested, you can go to theeducationdoctor.com/whattoknow to get $100 discount for the Kranse program
- Number2.com–free ACT help.

Chapter 8
Senior Year (Apply)

Your teen's senior year will start before you know it's here. Even as early as the summer, college applications will be ready for your teen. All the attention that your teen gets from colleges during his/her senior year is focused on getting him/her to apply. Here are some of the enticements your teen may receive:

- Invitations for an overnight visit
- College representatives hosting talks at your teen's high school
- Increased mailings of brochures
- Invitations to apply with no fee, no essay, no recommendation

The college invitations tend to be more about getting an increased number of applications rather than admitting your teen because your teen is a good fit for their campus community. So your teen should temper his/her excitement about these colleges and only apply if the college is truly a fit for him/her. It would be even better if your teen had already researched the college and intends to apply. In other words, just because your teen is *invited*, does not mean that he/she is *admitted*!

• Invitations for an Overnight Visit

If your teen is invited to stay overnight and has all expenses paid, then it may be worth considering, certainly if the college is already on your teen's list. Generally, your teen would have to apply for the all-expenses paid overnight visits. Those "fly-in" programs are usually reserved for first-generation or underrepresented students. (Learn more about "fly-in" programs in the bonus section at the end of this chapter.)

• College Representatives Visiting High School

When college representatives visit his/her high school, it's an opportunity for your teen to get questions answered and learn more specifics about the college campus. I often suggest that students learn more about the representatives' experience at a campus if a representative is an alum. That's the kind of information that's not available on the website. Meeting with a college rep at school does not replace a campus visit and should not be misconstrued as an offer of admission to that college.

Sometimes, college representatives will interview applicants during their visits to a high school. If your teen hasn't already submitted some information to express interest in a college, then your teen may not be invited to interview. And again, even if your teen is invited to interview, it doesn't mean that it will increase his/her chances of admissions. My son was told that his interview with a college rep at his high school was the "best interview of all the candidates," yet my son was denied admission. (It can be a challenge to temper your senior's desire to get through this process as quickly as possible and accept the first letter of admissions or limit your teen's options sooner than necessary.)

• Increased Mailings

Your mailbox will be inundated with college marketing materials. The mailed brochures that my son received were especially overwhelming during his senior year. In several cases, the same college would send 2-3 mailings a month from August to February. Most of the colleges had not been on my son's lists and would not have been a good fit had he applied and been admitted. For example, my oldest son was very clear that he preferred a more urban campus, especially since he attended high school in a rural community. About half of the colleges that mailed him brochures were located in rural communities from areas of the country that he had not considered previously. (See the book, *There Is Life After College* by Jeffrey J. Selingo; it tells about the importance of location in the college search.) Sending all those brochures to my son was a waste and inconsiderate.

- **Invitations to Apply with No Fee, No Essay, No Recommendation (FastApps)**

The expedited applications, known as FastApps, are the most insensitive attempts to lure prospective senior applicants. What I've noticed among my students who get these "Fast App" emails is that they tend to be students with lower GPAs and/or lower test scores. Each student who applied through the FastApp option still received a denial letter from that college.

Help but Don't Do in Senior Year

The fall of the senior year will be almost exclusively focused on college applications. This is the time when students can make decisions about application deadlines, i.e. Early Action, Early Decision, or Regular Decision (discussed in detail below). Students who are considering earlier deadlines should prepare their applications as soon as possible in their senior year. If students will participate in any optional admission interviews, these will also happen in the fall.

Seniors have a lot to juggle, i.e., studying through senior course load, applying to colleges, traveling for campus visits/interviews, retaking any tests, plus all the senior to-dos like headshots! At home, the arguments about college are likely to increase during the senior year. Be prepared for heightened tension and stress in your home particularly through the holidays. Here's why...

In late November and December, your teen's classmates who applied early will learn their admissions decisions. Whether those classmates were admitted or not will become outsized in the rumors around campus. Your teen, and maybe even parents, will hear such tales as:

- "She had a perfect score on the ACT but still didn't get into x college."
- "He got a full ride to x college."

In either case, there's so much more to the story and neither decision for another classmate has any bearing on your teen's chances of admissions. These early admissions outcomes, however, can be quite upsetting for all the other teens who have no idea what their classmate's submitted application actually looked like and what had a bearing on the decision they received. The most common reaction I see around this time frame is that the students who have not been admitted will randomly start applying to any college, especially ones on the CommonApp.

It will be very tempting for you to take action for your teen during his/her senior year, given all his/her extra responsibilities. Not only that, these additional responsibilities will often have strict deadlines and financial implications. Once YOU take action on behalf of your teen, it will hurt your teen's chances of getting in and getting money for college. Here are important things for you to know about your teen's senior year so that you can be helpful in supporting your teen but not doing the work yourself:

- Register a parent account on the CommonApp
- Budget for senior year expenses
- Know application deadlines

Get CommonApp Account

Parents should register for an account on the CommonApp. However, a parent account is not linked to his/her teen's account, but it does help to demystify the CommonApp. The parent can then see what information is requested in the application and support his/her teen with meeting the deadlines.

Before I go further, I want to make sure that I answer one of the most commonly asked questions... "What is the Common App?"

> The CommonApp is an undergraduate college admission application that applicants may use to apply to any of 731 member colleges and universities in 48 states and the District of Columbia as well as in Canada, China, and many European countries. The CommonApp makes it easy for students to apply to any college on the CommonApp system because all of the CommonApp data is in one place. Certainly, if a college does not require any additional essays or extra uploads, it's just a matter of clicking "Submit."

If you'd like to learn more about the CommonApp, please check out one of my most popular podcast episodes entitled "What Parents must know about the CommonApp." You can listen to the podcast at theeducationdoctor.com/whattoknow. (The purpose of this podcast series is to educate, equip and encourage parents. I personally am a huge fan of listening to podcasts during drive times and created this podcast for parents like myself who enjoy listening and learning as well.)

Anticipate Senior Year Expenses

Senior year expenses will add up quickly. In addition to the typical costs incurred during your teen's senior year such as photos, prom, and senior trips, there are college application fees to budget as shown below:

- **Individual College Applications.** These fees can range from $35 to apply to an HBCU (Historically Black College and University) or $75 for Northeastern University. My oldest son applied to 12 colleges (long story short, he panicked like so many other seniors) and by the time his last application was submitted in January of his senior year, we had spent $910 in college application fees. If your teen receives free and/or reduced lunch or participates in a special college-readiness program, then your teen may obtain a fee waiver. When I applied to college back in the 1980s, I requested a fee waiver from my school counselor and got one for all sixteen colleges where I applied. I'm not sure how generous your school counselor may be, but it's worth it for your teen to ask... all the school counselor can do is say "no" to your teen's request.

- **Official Test Scores.** Each college that requires an ACT or SAT score must receive an official score report directly from ACT or College Board for the SAT. Even if your teen self-reports their scores on the CommonApp or the college's own application system, the official score report from the testing agency is still required. In the 2017-18 school year, submitting an ACT score costs $12 (priority $16.50) and SAT is $12 (priority $31). If your teen reports an SAT score to 12 colleges, as my son did, then that will be $144. My son was a major procrastinator back then, but fortunately, he did not have to send any rush/priority SAT scores!

- **CSS Profile Application Fees.** CSS (College Scholarship Service) Profile is a financial aid application required by some colleges to determine your teen's eligibility for institutional scholarships. (In the next chapter on "Know your options to pay for college," I will say more about CSS Profile.) Not to be confused with FAFSA which is free, the CSS Profile costs $25 for one college and $16 for each additional college. In the case of my son, eight of his twelve colleges required submission of a CSS Profile, so the total cost was $137.

Know Your Teen's Application Deadlines

I highly recommend that you add your teen's college and financial aid application deadlines to your family and mobile calendars as soon as determined. Once your teen's college list is finalized, it's important to determine which deadline your teen will meet based on those offered. The college application deadlines may be as follows (in order of restrictiveness):

- **Regular/Rolling Admissions.** This is the standard deadline for all colleges. There are no restrictions on who can apply during the regular decision deadlines. Applicants to the "regular" deadline will not typically learn the admission decision until winter/spring of senior year. A "rolling" application deadline, however, means that admissions decisions are made as the applications are received. If a college has a "rolling" admissions program, then students may learn the admissions decision as soon as 2-3 weeks after submitting an application.

- **Early Action (EA).** Early Action is not restrictive, nor is it binding. I typically recommend that students apply to at least 2-3 colleges for the Early Action deadline. Students will find out by mid-December the college's admission decision: Admitted, Denied, or Deferred to Regular Deadline. If your teen gets an EA Admitted Decision, they do not have to respond to the college until the spring. It may take some pressure off your teen, but your teen should still continue to keep his/her options open and wait to receive all financial decisions. If your teen gets an EA Denied Decision, then it's good early information so your teen can keep things moving by applying to other colleges. If that EA Denied Decision came from a selective college, then your teen may want to double-check that his/her college list isn't too over-subscribed with selective colleges, i.e., balance out his/her list. The EA "Deferred" Decision means that a student's application decision will not be made until all Regular Decision Applications have been received. I strongly dislike EA Deferred Decisions because I think they unnecessarily drag out the stress of admissions, and in some cases, give students a false sense of hope that their application will be admissible. In short, there is no real downside to applying for Early Action, and it encourages teens to get an early start on the applications.

- **Restrictive Early Action.** All the details of this application's deadlines are similar as above except that the college may restrict an applicant to only applying to one college under the Early Action deadline. During the 2017-18 school year, these colleges had REA (Restricted Early Action) programs: Boston College, Harvard, Princeton, Stanford, Yale.

- **Early Decision.** This is the most restrictive admissions deadline, so I want to be crystal clear in stating its serious intent:

EARLY DECISION IS A BINDING, LEGAL CONTRACT.

If your teen applies Early Decision and is admitted, then your teen must attend the college, regardless of any financial award. With that being said, if your teen applies through Early Decision, YOU must sign off on the application stating that you realize that your teen is applying Early Decision. Your signature on the application confirms that you are aware that the application decision is binding and that you will be responsible for paying for the cost of attendance whether or not any financial aid is awarded. The school counselor is also notified that your teen has applied under the Early Decision program to ensure that your teen is only applying to one ED college. Be prepared, because if your teen is admitted under ED, the enrollment deposit is typically due two weeks after notification. Your teen must also withdraw any other applications immediately and will not have the benefit of learning other college decisions or negotiating the financial award offer. Early decision is serious and not to be "played with"!

The financial aid application deadlines can vary based on your teen's college application deadline. For example, if your teen applies to a college under Early Decision, then the financial aid application deadlines will be due within 1-2 weeks later. Colleges, like the University of Southern California, have an earlier college application deadline for students who want to be considered for merit-based scholarships.

Apply A+ Attitudes™ in 12th Grade

Your senior must have complete ownership of the college application process and use solid organizational skills whether they've been developed or not. In other words, your senior will have to "grow up."

It will take time and energy to get through the senior year. I don't mean to be too harsh in my words, but I see too many seniors who are just plain lazy. Their laziness costs parents a lot of time, money, and stress. This is why it's so important for parents to recognize the laziness long before a teen's senior

141

year and do something about it. The senior year has a way of magnifying the laziness and bringing out the worst kind of codependency that will limit the opportunities for a teen to mature and become independent. There are so many details to the application process that a lazy senior will either flounder and reach far less than his/her best potential or have a worn-down parent who does the work for them. A greater downside to the parent doing the work is that teens become resentful and still tend to flounder after leaving high school.

A key focus for the senior applying to college–owning the next phase of his/her life!

As I've already stated in the previous section, the work of applying to colleges must be done by the student, not the parent. This ownership goes far beyond owning the college application process... it's about recognizing that so much of what happens or not in your teen's senior year is about the next phase of your teen's life. If there's no ownership, i.e., responsibility during the senior year, then it sets a bad precedent.

The senior roadmap will keep you aware of what's happening in the college application process. If you are just starting the college admissions process, stay encouraged but realize that your teen has a lot of responsibilities ahead in the upcoming weeks. Your role is to support, help when necessary, and make sure that your teen is putting forth far more time and effort than you.

For each month of the senior year roadmap, make sure your teen follows through on each task outlined in addition to any other tasks that must be done. College application and financial aid deadlines are unforgiving. So, if your teen misses a deadline in his/her senior year, his/her opportunity to apply is gone. Again your role throughout this roadmap is to support your teen in meeting the overall deadlines for his/her college and financial aid applications.

As you review and take action with this senior guide, think of me as partnering and coaching you along your teen's educational journey. If you get stuck at any point during the senior year, my firm offers senior assessments, group coaching programs especially for parents with seniors, and emergency senior essay packages. You may contact me by email, drpamela@theeducationdoctor.com or at my website, theeducationdoctor.com, for more information and details on upcoming programs.

How to Do 12th Grade with Your Teen Month-by-Month

August

❖ **Your teen should set up his/her 12th grade roadmap for the school year.** There's a sample roadmap at the end of this chapter or you may download a printable version at this link: (theeducationdoctor.com/whattoknow). The printable roadmap, from my website, includes one actionable tip for each month with space for you to add other events or actions throughout the year. When you provide an email address to get the printable roadmap online, you will also receive additional bonus tips and notifications about upcoming events, such as programs for parents with seniors. To get the most of your teen's roadmap, please post a printed roadmap where your teen can see it regularly and stay on top of deadlines.

❖ **Update activities resume.** Now's a great time for your teen to update his/her activities resume with any summer experiences, while it's still fresh in mind. Updating the activities resume now will make it easier to quickly upload as a college application supplement and/or copy the text to paste directly into the CommonApp or other college applications.

❖ **Start drafting CommonApp essay.** Your teen should aim to have at least a first draft of the CommonApp essay started by the time school starts. There are several prompts for your teen to consider, then submit an essay for only one prompt. The essay must be 250-650 words. I urge you to encourage your teen to be very thoughtful about which CommonApp essay prompt he/she chooses. Many students shortchange themselves by only drafting one of the prompts. Giving each prompt careful consideration means that a student should actually be spending some time drafting each prompt in order to determine which essay response will be his/her best.

❖ **Determine 1-2 goals for 12th grade year.** Based on reviewing the senior roadmap and considering what your teen wants to achieve prior to spring graduation, your teen should be ready to set 1-2 goals for this school year. Examples of goals for 12th grade may be:

- Meet with one teacher two times per month to review class discussion and/or graded assignments.

- Get elected or selected for a leadership role in a club.

- Earn 95%+ score in three core courses for the year.

- *Continue* twenty hours volunteering with a community agency where your teen is already known/respected by the staff (note the word "continue" because fall of senior year is not the time to introduce new time commitments).

- Limit job hours to 10 per week to meet all college application deadlines.

❖ **Confirm courses.** Review the course schedule for the entire year to ensure that the right classes are included. Any adjustments should be based on necessary changes to meet high school course requirements of a college on your teen's list. If your teen is unable to get his/her top choice course selections, let your teen take the lead on determining whether to stick with the course or petition to switch his/her schedule.

September

❖ **Set calendar dates to meet with college reps during visits to high school.** The school counselor should have a listing of dates when college representatives will visit your teen's high school. Encourage your teen to meet college representative(s) during those visits if:

- The visit doesn't interfere with class participation.

- The college is already on your teen's list or could realistically be on his/her list. (Senior year is not the time for your teen to have an initial meeting with colleges where the majority of students applying have test scores and GPAs well above your teen... it's a waste of time.)

❖ **Actively participate in class discussions.** Active engagement in class discussion should be second nature to any college-bound high school senior. Class participation includes asking questions, volunteering for an activity, and/or making comments that add to the discussion.

❖ **Stay on top of the senior course workload.** Colleges will still request mid-year course grades, so this is no time for your teen to coast in his/her studies. The senior year courses can still be just as challenging as junior year. And if your teen attends a high school that ranks, then there will be even more pressure on your teen in his/her senior year to keep up the good work he/she has already been doing. With the time demands of college applications, your teen should stay ahead as much as possible because if he/she falls behind, it will take even more time and effort to catch up.

October

❖ **Finalize college list.** You and your teen should discuss his/her final list of colleges and the respective application deadlines. While your teen may feel confident in applying to colleges within a narrow selectivity range, i.e., too many "wild card" colleges that have admissions rates of less than 15% or only colleges with a greater than 70% chance of admissions, please encourage your teen to have a balanced list. A balanced list would be one with 3-4 colleges in each of these admissions ranges:

- Less than 30% admissions rate
- Between 30-70% admissions rate
- Greater than 70% admissions rate

❖ **Confirm financial aid application deadlines.** Since FAFSA opens October 1, now is a good time to start the application using the prior year tax return data.

❖ **Determine special talent submission, i.e., video, audio, writing.** If your teen has a special talent that he/she wants to share with an admissions committee, there are numerous opportunities for him/her to do so. Some colleges will accept a video, audio recording, creative portfolio, or written publication. Your teen should be sure to determine whether his/her submission will be considered and read all details about how to upload any additional supplement, if the college accepts them.

❖ **Confirm dates with recommenders and guidance staff for submitting reports and transcripts.** Your teen should follow-up with recommenders and school counselor to make sure that all documents are submitted on time. A good rule of thumb is to confirm with recommenders and school counselor at least two weeks prior to the first early application deadline. Colleges will not review incomplete applications so it's best for your teen to be diligent about getting documents submitted from teachers and school counselor.

November

❖ **Submit Early Action application and official ACT/SAT test scores to 1-3 colleges.**

❖ **Preview all merit award essays and begin drafting.** Some colleges will have specific essay requirements for scholarship applications. Your teen can check the colleges' websites for these details.

December

❖ **Finalize college applications and merit aid essays.**

❖ **Submit score reports from test agency to all remaining colleges.** It will be easier to remember now if your teen goes to the ACT or SAT website and submits a score report for each college with December-March deadlines.

❖ **Watch for moodiness.** Your teen may become particularly stressed and overwhelmed by looming college application deadlines and/or overhearing his/her classmates' application decisions. Now's the time for you to keep tempers down as much as possible. One way to do this may be to limit conversations about college admissions, especially with other family members during any holiday get-togethers.

January

❖ **Finalize college applications and merit aid essays.**

❖ **Learn more about the financial aid process.** Your teen should know even more about the financial aid process than you. Once your teen is in college, all financial aid renewal information will go directly to him/her (not to you), so your teen should learn now the importance of meeting deadlines and the type of financial aid documentation that you must submit on their behalf.

❖ **Check grade reports and submit mid-year reports.** Depending on term grades and teacher comments, your teen should use this feedback to decide on his/her next steps for the remainder of the school year. If your teen's grades are strong and match with a strong effort, then the next step is to continue with what he/she has already been doing. If your teen's grades are weak, i.e., below his/her goal, then the next step is to get immediate help from any resource that will make a difference in him/her improving his/her grade. Your teen can determine which colleges require midterm grade reports and then confirm with his/her school counselor to have the reports submitted. If the school counselor cannot send them, then your teen can contact the college to find out how he/she can send his/her own midterm report.

February

❖ **Monitor application status.** Your teen should expect to receive a confirmation from each college stating that his/her application is ready for review. If your teen does not receive such a confirmation, please have him/her contact the college right away to find out if there are any missing documents or additional information needed to complete his/her application. Your teen must be diligent in this regard because an incomplete application translates to a "Denied" application decision.

March

❖ **Avoid "senioritis" as best as possible.** Spring of the senior year is a tempting time for your teen to get anxious for the school year to end and start acting like it HAS ended. This "senioritis" is a well-documented issue and I see it every year among my students, which leads to the next action item...

❖ **Avoid making bad choices.** If your teen isn't careful about his/her attitude and behaviors, there's a chance that his/her admissions offers can be suspended or rescinded. Examples of bad choices include failing senior year grades, inappropriate social media posts, criminal activity, or other violations to a prospective college's code of conduct. It can happen and does every year... you just don't want your teen to be the example!

April

❖ **Attend admit weekends.** Almost every college will offer a special time for your teen to visit campus if he/she has been admitted. I believe that the "Admitted Student" visit is when the college decision is made. Every spring, students are surprised by the experience of an admitted student visit and make their final decision before they even return home from the visit.

Case in point: One of my students had been admitted to his dream college. His mother had attended the same college, and he had visited the campus several times over the years. The selective admissions of this college also impressed upon him that all his "hard work had paid off." This student was so assured that he wanted to attend this college that he was somewhat reluctant to even apply to other colleges and thought that the revisit for admitted students would take too much time away from his AP exam prep. Well, the short of the story is that my student visited his dream college as an admitted student and promptly decided that it wasn't the school for him after all. He ended up choosing another college that he also visited as an admitted student, one where he felt more comfortable.

May

❖ **Notify colleges of your decision and send a deposit to one.** When your teen signs the Common Application or any college application, he/she agrees to send a deposit to only one institution. "Double-depositing" is an ethical violation to that agreement. Your teen should re-read the application policy if his/her indecisiveness is a concern.

❖ **Advanced Placement tests.** If your teen has taken AP course(s) this year, then he/she will likely take any AP exam(s) during the first two weeks of May. (Some high schools mandate that your teen take the AP test(s) if he/she is enrolled in the course(s) but may waive this rule for a senior.) See sample schedule of AP exams on pages 130-131 or you may check my website (theeducationdoctor.com) and search for "AP test dates" to find the current schedule for your senior.

June

❖ Congratulations to your proud GRADUATE!

July

❖ Enjoy summer and get ready for Freshman year!

Bonus

COMPASS

Senior Monthly Roadmap

In addition to this Roadmap to Get In Get Money™ for college, you will receive weekly update emails with additional real-time tips to add to this checklist. I would love to partner with you to achieve your teen's educational vision. Please contact me today - drpamela@theeducationdoctor.com

August
- ☐ Start drafting application essays
- ☐ _____

September
- ☐ Determine scholarship strategy and set submission deadlines
- ☐ _____

October
- ☐ Confirm deadlines with recommenders and guidance staff
- ☐ _____

November
- ☐ Submit EA application(s)
- ☐ _____

December
- ☐ Finalize college applications and merit aid essays
- ☐ _____

January
- ☐ Finalize college applications and merit aid essays
- ☐ _____

February
- ☐ Submit prior year tax documentation
- ☐ _____

March
- ☐ Monitor application status
- ☐ _____

April
- ☐ Determine re-visit and waitlist plan, if needed
- ☐ _____

May
- ☐ Notify colleges of your decision and send deposit to one
- ☐ _____

June: **CONGRATULATIONS ON YOUR GRADUATION!!!**

Pamela Ellis, The Education Doctor®, has helped thousands of teens attend a college that feels like home. She brings 25 years of experience in education to assist with college selection, admissions, financial aid, and freshman transition success. Dr. Pamela holds a PhD from Stanford and MBA from Dartmouth. For tips and insight to help your college-bound teen, visit compasscollegeadvisory.com.

Copy and post this checklist to keep track of expectations and actions to navigate 12th grade year.

Bonus: College Application Organizer

Use this handy guide to keep track of deadlines and application details in one place:

	College 1	College 2	College 3
Decision plan (EA, REA, RD, Rolling)			
Application deadline			
Interview sign-up			
Interview			
Common app supplements			
Supplementary materials			
Other notes			

Bonus: Tips and Resources for Seniors

College Survival Books

- How to Win at College: Surprising Secrets for Success from the Country's Top Students by Cal Newport
- The Naked Roommate: And 107 Other Issues You Might Run Into in College by Harlan Cohen
- U Chic: College Girls' Real Advice for Your First Year (and Beyond!) by Christie Garton

Fly-Ins

If your teen is first-generation or minority/under represented, then a "fly-in" may be an opportunity to visit a college with all expenses paid. Here are the steps *your teen can take* to find out about colleges that offer these opportunities and apply:

- Ask school counselor about colleges who offer these programs.
- Search online at greenlight.com for their latest listing of fly-in programs or do a Google search with specific words like this phrase: "high school senior fly-in college visit."
- Complete applications by the deadlines. Some colleges will have deadlines as early as June for a fall fly-in.

Gap/Bridge Year Programs

A "gap/bridge year" program is one offered in the period between completing high school and beginning college. It can be either a semester or a full year program. A purpose of these programs is to support teens with being productive while they prepare for the next phase of their life. These gap/bridge year programs are worth considering if your teen is not ready to go to college for whatever reason. I have worked with teens who weren't ready for college for these reasons:

- Lack of maturity
- Needed to be more independent from their parents
- Had some social and/or emotional needs to address before transitioning to college
- Wanted to qualify for a Division 1 athletic program in their sport
- Needed more academic preparation

There has been increasing interest and participation in gap/bridge year programs. In his book, *There Is Life After College,* the author, Jeffrey J. Selingo, discusses several programs. Likewise, you can search online for programs and/or check out one of these programs to learn more:

- Americorps
- Global Citizen Year
- Thinking Beyond Borders
- USA Gap Year Fair (hosted across major US cities)
- Where There Be Dragons

The Education Doctor® Podcasts

These podcast episodes are relevant for senior year:

- "What Parents Must Know about the Common Application"
- "5 College Admissions Deadlines Every Parent Must Understand"
- "How to Help Your Teen Write Better"

You can listen at theeducationdoctor.com/whattoknow

Part III
Letting Go with Grace

Interlude:
A Note to Parents on Transition

No matter how well you prepare for your teen to reach his/her college dreams academically and socially, it will be a big transition for you as well. Even as a parent who has helped hundreds of teens get into their top choice colleges and get an average of $75,000 in scholarships, it was emotionally difficult for me to handle my own children going away to college.

My oldest son attended Georgetown University which is a short plane ride or seven-hour drive from our Ohio home. I was very nervous as his first days of college drew near and made sure that we spent plenty of time together as a family. (This may have been a bit too smothering at times, but I hope not.)

Once we dropped him off at college, I missed him terribly. Even during the orientation weekend, I felt that he had a much busier and much more independent life than when he was in high school. Although my son had attended a boarding school, there were a lot of checks in place and a notification system to parents if students were away from campus unsupervised for any reason.

I was shocked to learn during his freshman year that he once traveled from DC to Philadelphia on his own without the knowledge of anyone at Georgetown. My son was a college student now, so I didn't get any direct calls or emails from anybody at his college about anything related to grades, on-campus activities, let alone his off-campus whereabouts.

If I had known beforehand that he was traveling, then it only would have caused me to worry unnecessarily.

It was time for me to learn how to let go a bit more.

When it comes to being able to let your teen go to college with grace, it's about possessing these A+ Attitudes™ that will best position you to help your teen through to college completion:

- A+ Attitudes™ #4 – Know your options to pay for college.

- A+ Attitudes™ #5 – Be present for freshman year.

Chapter 9
A+ Attitudes™ #4 – Know Your Options to Pay for College

The rising cost to attend college is on the minds of families everywhere. There's even a lot of debate about whether college is "worth it." If you're reading this book, then I assume you agree with me that college is valuable. While I won't necessarily argue about the value proposition of higher education and whether the return on investment is "worth it," I will share that I believe that college can be affordable. The first two parts of this book focused on how college can be achievable, which started with this mindset:

- A+ Attitudes™ #1 – It's All about Fit
- A+ Attitudes™ #2 – There's a Lot of Money Out There
- A+ Attitudes™ #3 – Distance Doesn't Matter

This chapter in the third part of the book will focus on what families must know and the mindset to make college affordable.

- A+ Attitudes™ #4 – Know Your Options to Pay for College

The first thing that every family must realize is that you must apply in order to qualify for financial aid and/or scholarships. This may sound basic, but I'm making it clear that parents and students must apply for financial aid and/or scholarships in order to get them. Every year families miss the deadlines. In short, if you do not complete the financial statement forms or your teen doesn't complete required essays and get them in before the college's deadlines, then you can expect to pay the sticker price for college which isn't "affordable" for 98% of the families who want their teen to attend college. No one likes or wants to pay full price, so we will review ways that you can have college funded through other means than your own checkbook.

Make Time for This Balanced Conversation

It is critical that you discuss college expenses with your teen early and often, including who will pay for what. Perhaps even a generation ago, this conversation might never have taken place. Today, however, it is imperative given the rising costs of attending college.

These discussions can start as early as middle school since students have developed a sense of value by then and are already exposed to these conversations through media anyway. In middle school, the conversation may center around potential scholarship opportunities. Many scholarships that you may find on the websites listed have a minimum age of thirteen years for eligibility. Typically, these scholarship awards will follow the student to whichever college they attend.

By the time, your teen is in high school, the "college expense" discussion may center around general financial literacy and how college can be funded through various sources. Please avoid having these conversations as a basis for your teen to build his/her college list. What I mean by those words of caution is simply this... *the sticker price does not determine the college list.*

I refer to colleges having a "sticker price" because of the similarities with automobiles. Both have high sticker prices and both are discounted based on the purchaser. Since you are likely familiar with the car buying scenario, I will elaborate on how this sticker price analogy applies to colleges:

Many private colleges are priced higher than in-state tuition at a public college. However, the private colleges may offer more scholarships and awards that significantly reduce what a family will pay to attend, i.e. the college is applying a discount. Overall, only 20% of families pay the full cost of attendance. The other 80% are getting some form of financial aid and/or scholarships that "discount" the cost of attendance posted on the website. (Check the average tuition paid on the college's website and compare the difference.)

Now let's discuss how you can be part of the 80%.

Know Where the Money Is

Money for college comes in various forms. This table shows the type of money available for college and the four primary sources.

	Federal	State	External	Colleges
Grants	$	$	$	$
Scholarships	$	$	$	$
Work-study	$			
Loans			$	$

A key similarity of grants and scholarships is that they do not have to be paid back. Although the terms may be used interchangeably, there is a key difference between grants and scholarships. "Grants" are usually need-based which means that a family must demonstrate a financial need to receive the financial award to pay for college. The term "scholarship" applies to merit-based awards that are distributed regardless of whether a family "needs" additional financial assistance. (Your teen can get a scholarship for almost anything, even before senior year of high school.) My aim in elaborating on

161

the types and sources of college money is that it will help you learn where the money is and what you must do to support your teen in accessing these funds.

Grants Are About Your Income

Sources of grants for your teen are:

- Federal and state governments
- Nonprofit organizations
- Colleges

• Federal and State Grants

One of the most well-known federal grants is the Pell Grant. Pell is available for undergraduates who do not already have a bachelor's degree. Pell Grants go to students with an annual family income of $50,000 or less. The total amount of Pell money for colleges is determined by government funding. The maximum amount that a student can receive for a Pell Grant in the 2017-18 school year is $5,920. If your teen qualifies for a Pell Grant, you can think of this grant as a "pass-through" in that the money goes directly to the college where your teen enrolls.

Another federal grant available is the Federal Supplemental Educational Opportunity Grant (FSEOG) program, which is also determined by EFC. This grant is awarded to students who still have an additional need beyond the Pell Grant award. FSEOG grants range between $400 and $4,000 per year. The total amount of FSEOG money available at a college is determined by the financial aid office where your teen enrolls.

All states and the District of Columbia offer their own grants paid for by property taxes and lottery funds. State grants can be similar to an FSEOG in that they are awarded if students have an additional need beyond the Pell Grant. The amounts awarded per student will vary. The criteria for these grants may vary as well. For example, Ohio awards range from $1,500 to $5,700, with funds designated for STEM majors, dependents of police or firefighters, or even former residents of the state. Residents of Arizona can qualify for a grant up to $2,500 per year after twelve months of living in that state. Interestingly, for one of the Arizona grants, the funds are paid directly to the student, rather than the college.

• Nonprofit Organizations

Almost every community has a nonprofit organization (or several in larger cities) that offers grants for students to attend college. The total amount awarded is based on contributions and/or endowed funds. There will usually be a separate application that your teen must submit to the nonprofit organization in order to be considered for their grants. Even if the name of the nonprofit program uses the word "scholarship" I refer to it as a grant here because the FAFSA (see description below) is generally used by these organizations to determine which applicants receive awards.

To illustrate, if your teen applies for a $1,000 grant from a local nonprofit foundation, then your teen would be eligible to receive the full award the foundation offers. However, if your EFC is higher than $0, the foundation could give your teen a partial grant or no grant at all. The foundation will usually have a budget for the total amount that can be distributed. For example, if the budget for the grant fund is $400,000 per year, then a maximum of 400 students could be awarded a $1,000 grant from the foundation.

• Colleges

The financial aid budget of a college determines how money is awarded each year to students who enroll. You can learn the financial aid budget for a specific college at its website. Each college may also allocate a portion of the budget for need-based awards. The amount that students receive is determined by FAFSA and in some cases, the College Scholarship Service (CSS Profile).

You can send a FAFSA report to any college by using their designated code. When you list a college code on the FAFSA, it allows the college to see your EFC results. If the FAFSA form does not have the college-specific code, then the college will not receive any verification that your family has completed FAFSA. No FAFSA means no financial aid will go to the college from the federal government, state government, or nonprofit organizations.

An important reason to send a FAFSA report to a college is that some colleges may guarantee to meet up to 100% of need, based on your EFC. What's interesting to note here is that your financial need is determined by the colleges based on the cost of attendance. Therefore, your "need" at one college can be different from the "need" at another college. You really can't know what the total award will be unless you apply. I reiterate this point about the importance of applying because every year I hear from parents that they don't want to apply through FAFSA because they think they won't qualify for any award.

> **Case in point:** One of my client families applied through FAFSA, even though their annual income was far above the $50,000 level. A college where their son applied actually awarded the family an additional $3,000 per year for filling out the FAFSA. So the return on their spending twenty minutes to complete FAFSA was well worth the $12,000 windfall.

What I say to parents every year is... "All they (the colleges) can do is say 'No'" So, fill out the FAFSA!

Families who apply for grants must complete FAFSA and sometimes the CSS Profile in order for their eligibility to be determined. Thus, your financial need may vary by college.

FAFSA

The Free Application for Federal Student Aid, "FAFSA," is a universal form that organizations use to determine eligibility for need-based grants. The FAFSA asks for basic financial information that is verified through tax filings. After completing the FAFSA, a family can learn their Expected Family Contribution, or EFC (Expected Family Contribution). The EFC can range from zero and up. An EFC of "$0" means that your family has the most financial need. A higher EFC would indicate that your FAFSA results showed that your family has the financial means to pay more for college.

CSS Profile

Another form that is usually required by private colleges or universities to determine financial need is the College Scholarship Service (CSS Profile). The CSS Profile is a product of College Board. (Yes, the same people who sell the SAT and Advanced Placement tests.) The CSS Profile is quite different from the FAFSA and may ask more detailed financial questions. Because each family's "need" is determined by the college, the CSS Profile includes questions specifically from the college. At the start of the form, you indicate the colleges that will receive the results. The CSS Profile is then populated with select questions from the specific colleges. For example, one client family was asked about the depreciation of her assets and auto payments. Another client family, with a different set of colleges, did not have any questions about asset depreciation schedules.

The time it takes to complete a CSS Profile can be up to an hour. If you have the following listed documents ready beforehand, then it can save time:

- Current federal income tax return(s), if completed
- Prior year federal income tax return(s)
- Most recent W-2 forms and other records of money earned

- Records of untaxed income and benefits for current and prior years
- Current bank statements
- Current mortgage information

If a college requires a CSS Profile, apply, regardless of whether you think you qualify. You may be surprised at what you get for applying!

Scholarships Are About Your Teen

Just as the name implies, merit-based awards are based on your teen's academic/intellectual/athletic or other accomplishments. These accomplishments are far-ranging and, again, vary based on who awards the scholarship. Merit scholarships can be offered by any organization, as well as the colleges themselves.

Starting early is the key to finding scholarships for college. I will explain further the merit scholarships from these sources so that you can understand better where to apply and what it takes to apply.

External (Corporate) Organizations

Outside or corporate scholarships provide resources from organizations other than colleges and universities. This means that the scholarship dollars follow the student to whichever college he/she attends.

At the national, state, and local levels, outside scholarships reward students for their artistic, written, oratorical, or sports prowess. Sometimes, they are even awarded to promote particular courses of study, like science or fine arts. Families can typically begin applying for outside scholarships as early as thirteen years of age. There are a number of websites that list these scholarships and how to apply throughout the year. There are also scholarships available locally through such organizations as Rotary, unions, employee associations, or other nonprofit groups.

One mom shook her head in disappointment as she spoke with me about all the hours she spent searching for scholarship money during her son's senior year of high school. The applications were due fairly early in the year, often requiring essays. Unfortunately, all the time she spent didn't amount to any scholarships because she and her teen started too late.

I refer to these type of scholarships as "lottery" scholarships because of the relatively low chances of "winning." When you look at the fine print text of the application instructions, you will read that the chances of winning are often based on the number of submissions. These scholarships are indeed quite competitive. Even for a prestigious scholarship like the Coca-Cola Scholarship, there are still thousands of students with perfect ACT/SAT scores and strong GPAs.

Instead of putting all your eggs in the outside scholarship basket, students should consider scholarships directly from colleges. That's where the really big money for college is found. For example, my students have received scholarship awards ranging from $40,000 to $300,000. These scholarships came directly from the colleges.

Colleges

About $40 billion is offered in merit scholarships directly from colleges, as compared to the $11 billion available in scholarships from external (corporate) sources. Students may, therefore, be better off applying and getting admitted to the colleges that offer merit scholarships.

Many of my client families with moderate to higher incomes may not have qualified for needs-based grants, yet they were still able to greatly reduce the expense of college through merit-based scholarships. These merit scholarships came directly from the colleges and universities.

Colleges are recruiting students that will contribute to their campus community in a myriad of ways. Even if a college seeks a certain type of student from a particular state, they can offer a "merit scholarship" to recruit/attract that student to their campus.

Here are five examples of the merit scholarships that my students have received and what they did to earn these awards:

CASE STUDY 1: Scholarship for Fine and Visual Arts– To obtain these awards, students submitted a portfolio as part of the application process. Much of their portfolio preparation was completed during the summer before senior year. Also, I encouraged them to attend a National Portfolio Day as a way to get feedback on their portfolio before they submitted it to colleges. Students took advantage of the National Portfolio Day to learn about potential colleges that they wanted to visit as well. The subsequent visit reinforced their interest in the colleges and further helped with securing the scholarship awards.

CASE STUDY 2: Scholarships to Travel Abroad–There are a number of scholarships offered by colleges that are posted on their websites and listed in my firm's online portal. My students have applied for a number of these scholarships. Several of them have been for travel funds to study abroad. Students submitted an essay discussing how they would benefit from traveling abroad as part of the application process. In most cases, these were short essays (100 words or less), which I think are harder to write than long essays (500 words or more)!

CASE STUDY 3: Scholarships to do Research with Faculty Mentors–There are several colleges that seek students who are interested in research, i.e. Clark University in Worcester, Massachusetts. My students who received these scholarships had all demonstrated their interest in research through summer experiences. The summer experiences included working in a laboratory, conducting research through a formal summer program offered at a university, and continuing a project with a high school teacher.

CASE STUDY 4: $100K+ Scholarships–These awards went to students who expressed interest in a specific department or program featured at that college. Students wrote about their interests in the supplemental essays and also each had demonstrated an interest in these particular areas through a summer experience. The department interests ranged from business to natural sciences to engineering. Several colleges required essays for a particular named scholarship and a few offered invitation-only interviews. Colleges are seeking different types of students and will offer scholarships to attract THAT type of student.

CASE STUDY 5: Scholarships for Being MALE—I don't know how else to say it but there's been a trend over the years where my male students get awarded more money just for being males. This is the only common attribute that I've found... some of them didn't even have the strongest GPA or high school resume. (Go figure, right?) A college admissions officer from a well-known Florida university even stated at a professional conference that:

We gather all the applications from males first, review their credentials, award scholarships, send them offers, and wait on their response. Then we look at the female application pool... Frankly, we need more males on our campuses.

Yes... I was shocked to hear this too. However, the fact that more females are enrolling in college means that a number of campuses have more females. Colleges that seek to reach a 50/50 gender balance will continue to award these male scholarships as needed.

Some colleges may require that students write an essay to express interest in receiving a particular merit scholarship. Your teen must be sure to meet any deadlines for scholarship writing requirements, in order to be considered. In other cases, students may only have to submit their college application in order to qualify. Colleges tend to do a good job of considering all merit scholarships available for a student, prior to sending any award notices. When a college wants your teen to attend, they will make an effort to make it affordable.

Work-Study Is Spelled J-O-B

The most misunderstood line item on a financial aid award letter is work-study. Work-study is a federally funded program to help students pay for college-related expenses (indirect costs) by working part-time. As a federally funded program, eligibility for work-study is determined by completing FAFSA.

What is misunderstood about this program is that students must enroll at the college and then find a job. The job can be on- or off-campus. The wages *earned* would be the work-study "award." The grant aspect of this program is that when a job is part of the work-study program, then the wages are paid by the federal government, rather than the place where the student is employed. It's essentially a pass-through. The best part about a work-study job is that the employer takes into account the student's course schedule.

If your teen does not qualify for work-study, then there may be other part-time jobs available on-campus that do not require a work-study award. For most students, especially freshmen it would be best to work on-campus to save time on commuting and work in an environment that is more understanding that academics come first.

Although I qualified for work-study during college, I decided to work off campus to earn a higher hourly rate. My first off-campus job in freshman year at Stanford was at a savings and loans bank. The money and time I spent on commuting far exceeded the higher dollar/hour wage. It was also a more stressful job than any I could have had on campus because the hours were very strictly 2 p.m.-6 p.m. M-F and 9 a.m.-1 p.m. Saturdays. This schedule did not accommodate my course load, exams, or any student activities. Overall, working off-campus in freshman year sacrificed my studies and grades.

Loans Aren't Evil

We have all read the statistics about the "student debt crisis" and how college graduates have loans in excess of $100,000. That does sound alarming. However, when we look more closely at this "crisis" then we can see that the excessive loans are largely drawn from students attending for-profit colleges. With 3,000+ nonprofit colleges with a range of admissions criteria and majors, it's really not necessary to even consider a for-profit college. Almost 90% of students attending for-profit colleges take out debt to pay for tuition and fees. Seven out of ten students at public or nonprofit colleges take on student debt.

The average loan debt amount is closer to $30,000 for students attending public or nonprofit colleges. The colleges may list this information on their website or you can check The Project on Student Debt annual report (ticas.org/posd/home). The amount of debt can vary greatly by college.

When I graduated from Stanford, my total loan debt was $10,000. Today, Stanford and several selective colleges have no-loan policies. Again if your teen gets admitted, he/she won't have to worry about student loan debt.

Another loan that gets overlooked though is PLUS Loan which is available to parents. It's the parents' decision whether they want to incur this debt, which may have a higher interest rate than a loan directly to the student. Likewise, there is no limit on the amount that a parent can borrow up to the total cost of attendance. In the cases where I have seen a PLUS Loan included in the financial award letter of my private clients, the students have had weaker GPAs. This was another way that families were penalized because the student didn't take his/her academics seriously through high school. Lack of early preparation will cost the family more financially later.

Stop Looking at Tuition

Too often, when parents are considering whether their teen should apply to a college, they look at the tuition first. This is quite misleading and short-changes a student's college options.

Case in point: One of my private students only wanted to apply to the flagship state university. It was a great institution, but most states have a budget crisis that keeps them from being able to award any scholarships at all. If I allowed the student to only apply to a college that looked less expensive online, then he would have missed all the great opportunities that came from the grants and scholarships that other institutions awarded to him. The flagship state university offered him NO award at all so the total bill would have been the total bill published online.

When looking at financial information on college websites, I recommend that parents and students consider these data points to get a better understanding of how college is paid for:

- Cost of attendance
- Financial statistics
- Institutional priorities

As I explain each data point, it may help illustrate why it's not always easy for families to know whether to apply to a college only based on the sticker price.

Cost of Attendance

Rather than looking at tuition only, families should understand the overall cost of attendance. The two types of costs are direct and indirect. Direct costs are paid directly to the college where your teen enrolls. An indirect cost is a college-related expense your teen/family pays to another business, i.e. bookstore, airline, etc.

Direct (paid to college)	Indirect (paid to others)
Tuition and fees Room and Board	Books and fees Personal expenses Transportation to college

Direct costs can be paid by grants, scholarships, and/or parents. Indirect costs are usually paid by the student and/or family. This is an important distinction that I didn't know as a first-generation college student. Back then, I thought that my grants and scholarships covered books as well. What a surprise when I went to buy my books freshman year at Stanford with $70 and the final bill was $350!

When your teen receives a grant or scholarship, the money typically goes directly to the college. The money is applied to the direct costs first. If there's any money left over, then your teen will receive a reimbursement.

Financial Statistics

Colleges will report on their website or through written documents quite a bit of financial information, like annual financial aid budget and other key statistics. Three data points that I think help demystify the whole conversation around college affordability are: 1) percent of need met, 2) average cost to attend, and 3) percentage of students receiving awards. These statistics show a college's financial generosity.

The percent of need met can range up to 100%. The colleges that meet 100% of need are often your most selective colleges, so your teen must also be able to get in, in order to qualify.

The average cost to attend can be compared to the direct costs. For example, Williams College has direct costs of $67,700. However, the average cost to attend was $15,800, far below the direct costs. The percentage of students receiving awards at Williams is about 50%. This is a good indication of there being economic diversity on campus as well.

Institutional Priorities

An "institutional priority" refers to what's important to that college. Just in the same way that your family has certain priorities and values, so do colleges. There's a saying that if you want to know what a person values, look at their checkbook, the same is true for a college, as well.

A great way to learn about the institutional priorities of a college is to look at where they are investing. If the college hires a new staff for first-generation students, then it's likely that recruiting and retaining first-generation students is a priority. If a new women's lacrosse field is being built, then that's a strong signal that women lacrosse players will be recruited to support that program.

In short, there's more to a college than its tuition.

Bonus: FAFSA Cheat Sheet

The Financial Aid season officially begins October 1 with the release of theFree Application for Student Aid, which is accepted by nearly all US colleges. Another form that is also used by colleges is the College Scholarship Service Profile, known by its acronym, CSS.

These forms are quite different. Please know that your family will complete these forms based on the colleges where your student applies. This summary table on answers the three most common questions about CSS and FAFSA:

	CSS Profile	FAFSA
Why should I apply?	This application is used to qualify families for **College-specific sources**	This application is used to qualify families for **Federal sources and College-specific sources**
How is the "need" calculated?	Assumes home equity, minimal student contribution, and calculation uses consumer price index	Assumes no student contribution and calculation uses federal standard of living guidelines
What does it cost to apply?	$25 for 1st college, $16 for each additional (Note: Automatic waiver for up to 8 colleges)	Free

Bonus: Strategies for Saving Time

1) Set up a PIN for FAFSA through this website http://www.pin.ed.gov/

2) Plan to do the CSS registration in one sitting! Keep the CSS ID number.

3) Complete the CSS first, then print an FAFSA worksheet to help with using the same data from the CSS Profile.

4) Complete CSS Profile and FAFSA at the latest by mid-January.

5) Have these documents ready:

   a) Current federal income tax return(s), if completed

   b) Prior year federal income tax return(s)

   c) Most recent W-2 forms and other records of money earned

   d) Records of untaxed income and benefits current and prior year

   e) Current bank statements

   f) Current mortgage information

   g) Records of savings, stocks, bonds, trusts, and other investments

6) Do not leave any blanks on the application. If not applicable, use "0."

7) Please remember to keep user name and password information for your student; it will be the same each year. If you have another child who will attend college, they will have a different user name and password when applying to college.

Bonus: Tips and Resources for Financial Aid and Scholarships

National Scholarships

- Coca Cola Foundation
- Intel Foundation
- QuestBridge
- The Jack Kent Cooke Foundation

NOTE: There are scholarship programs that award college scholarships to children who are under age thirteen and in grades eight and below. These scholarships can be difficult to locate due to privacy laws regarding children. They include, for example, the Christopher Columbus Community Service Awards which issues $2,000 savings bonds to winning team members of a competition focused on solving community problems with science and technology. Another is the Jif Most Creative Peanut Butter Sandwich Contest with a grand prize of $25,000. (Someone has to win it, right?) Find a list of these scholarships and more at: http://www.finaid.org/scholarships/age13.phtml

Useful Websites

- cappex.com
- finaid.org
- petersons.com
- unigo.com

Chapter 10
A+ Attitudes™ - Be Present for Freshman Year

Once your teen has started freshman year of college, there are ways for you to be a part of their college experience, but let go and trust that you have raised them to be responsible in the many decisions they will make during college. I recommend that you, when possible, do the following:

1) Encourage your teen to participate in pre-orientation events

2) Attend Freshman orientation

3) Attend Family Weekend

4) Help your teen move after Freshman year

Yes, I recognize that these latter options can be expensive to do, so I only suggest them if it's financially feasible.

Take the Opportunity to Bond Early

There will be a couple of opportunities for your teen to bond early with his/her classmates. You can support your teen with making these social ties early during the Admitted Student Visit and/or during the pre-orientation program.

I discussed the importance of the Admitted Student Visit in Chapter 8, "How to Do 12th Grade with Your Senior Month-by-Month" because I believe that is when the college decision is truly made to attend. My oldest son attended two Admitted Student Visits. One of the colleges he visited was ranked as his first choice and the other was Georgetown. Visiting the other college and meeting his future classmates left him very disappointed in his prospects of enjoying the next four years there. The Admitted Student Visit to Georgetown confirmed his academic and social interests in attending college there.

When I attended the Admitted Student Visits along with my son, there were opportunities for me to learn about the academic and social programs available for my son and hear from financial aid administrators. After attending the Admitted Student Visits, I felt more comfortable with my son's decision and better prepared to support him with the transition to the college of his choice.

A second way that your teen can bond early with one or two classmates is to attend a pre-orientation event. My son was notified of the pre-orientation programs early in the summer and had to submit a formal application to attend. A number of colleges offer these pre-orientation programs. If your teen will attend a college that offers a pre-orientation, please encourage him/her to apply to participate.

The pre-orientation can be very rewarding because your teen can meet other new students with similar interests, Because the pre-orientation programs are often limited in size, it can be a less intimidating way to make a friend or two and get some insider knowledge from upperclassmen who often lead these pre-orientation programs. My oldest son had a wonderful pre-orientation experience; he met a few new friends, got the inside scoop on professors, courses, special grant opportunities, and learned more about public transit and social needs of DC neighborhoods. Another benefit to his pre-orientation experience is that it raised his awareness of how he can make an impact in such a large urban community.

Freshman Orientation

Depending on the college that your teen attends, Freshman Orientation will be held during the summer or immediately prior to classes starting. If you are able to attend, I highly recommend that you consider participating in Freshman Orientation. There will be limited programming for parents during that time, but it's an opportunity for you to show your support to your teen.

When I attended Freshman Orientation for my oldest son, it took a bit of extra coordination and expenses. I mentioned in the prior section that my son attended a pre-orientation program. Because I wanted to take his younger siblings to see where he would be attending college, we all drove my elder son to DC for his pre-orientation program. Then a week later, we took a flight to DC to attend Freshman Orientation activities. There were still a lot of errands to run during that weekend for supplies and dorm furnishings. After living in his dorm room for a week during pre-orientation, my son learned what he should-have-packed and still-needed-to-buy.

Attending the parent activities during Freshman Orientation also allowed me to meet a couple of parents who had students in the freshman class. Exchanging phone numbers with them was a way to feel like I knew someone else who was going through a similar experience as myself. I kept in touch with one of the three moms I met that weekend. She's offered a helpful perspective when I had questions about Georgetown or her own experience of having her oldest teen go to college.

Family Weekend

Most colleges will have a weekend designated for families of freshmen to visit the campus during the school year. I suggest that you add "Family Weekend" at your teen's college to your calendar well in advance, especially if it's distant. Once you have the dates, make a hotel reservation immediately. Local hotels will fill up quickly during any campus-related event. I will book my DC hotels several months in advance to get a better deal on room rates.

The "Family Weekend" events are typically more extensive than Freshman Orientation programming. Because your teen will be so busy with classes and campus social life, expect to see him/her only briefly. With my son, I would meet him for a meal during my visits, but that would be the extent of our time together given the time demands of his course load. The point of my visit was to stay up-to-date on happenings at his university and learn more about his college experience. My visit was NOT about keeping him from being the best student he could be and enjoying the fun social activities that are so much interwoven in the college experience.

On a couple of visits, I was able to meet my son's new friends at college. These introductions were somewhat different than meeting his friends when he was in middle school. I didn't expect to meet their parents too and trusted that my son would make good choices about friendships.

I was able to see my son each month of Freshman Year. It took a lot of travel planning, schedule coordination, and more expenses. It was time and money well worth it for the peace of mind it gave me about his transition to college.

Move From the Dorm

Helping your teen move at the end of the freshman year may be necessary, depending on his/her summer plans. There will be storage available in the local area for your teen to store his/her belongings. Monthly storage costs can be expensive, but your teen will likely be able to find other students he/she can share storage space with over the summer. Your help may be needed to move the belongings to storage and/or move belongings back to your home.

My oldest son had a summer job in DC after freshman year so he stored some of his belongings in DC and brought the rest back home to Ohio. We drove to DC from Ohio to help him move because it would have been more expensive for him to fly home with all the items he had to move. (During the time when my son returned to Ohio for three weeks, he applied for a couple of scholarships with a June deadline. I mentioned this so that you will remind your teen that there are many scholarships available once they are in college.)

I recently heard a mom remark that each move for the next school year decreases. So, for all the things my son moved out of his dorm, my hope is that we will move fewer items into his sophomore dorm. I don't want to repeat the experience of the freshman move out... too much stuff! It takes time, money, and energy to assist your college student with these moves.

Bonus: Sample Packing List for College Freshman

Sample Packing List
for
College Freshman

BASICS:
- BACKPACK
- POSTERS/ DRY ERASE BOARD & MARKERS/ CALENDAR
- STATIONARY/ ADDRESS BOOK /STAMPS
- HAT/ GLOVES/ SCARF/ WARM COAT
- UMBRELLA
- SEWING KIT/ SMALL TOOL KIT
- PLASTIC FOOD STORAGE CONTAINERS
- STORAGE CRATES
- SILVERWARE/ CAN OPENER
- SPORTS EQUIPMENT/ BIKE & U LOCK
- PHOTOS/ CAMERA
- DICTIONARY /THESAURUS
- MICROWAVE-SAFE DISHES & MUGS
- IRON/ IRONING BOARD
- AREA RUG
- STICKYTACK (NO NAILS)
- GAMES/ PLAYING CARDS
- SMALL SAFE

LAUNDRY & CLEANING SUPPLIES:
- LAUNDRY BAG
- LAUNDRY DETERGENT/ DRYER SHEETS
- HANGERS
- DISHWASHING SOAP
- STAIN REMOVER
- CLEANING SUPPLIES/ PAPER TOWELS
- BROOM/ DUST PAN
- AIR FRESHENER

CONNECTIVITY:
- DEVICE -TO - DEVICE

EMERGENCY SUPPLIES:
- FIRST AID KIT
- HEALTH INSURANCE INFO/ MEDICATIONS
- FLASHLIGHT WITH EXTRA BATTERIES
- WRITTEN LIST OF EMERGENCY CONTACTS

BED & BATH ITEMS:
- BED SHEETS (TWIN EXTRA LONG 80")
- BLANKETS
- PILLOWS/ PILLOWCASES
- BEDSPREAD
- TOWELS/ WASHCLOTHS
- FLIP FLOPS/ SHOWER TOTE
- SLIPPERS/ ROBE
- SOAP/ SHAMPOO & CONDITIONER
- HAIRSTYLING PRODUCTS/ HAIR DRYER/ CURLING OR FLAT IRON
- TOOTHBRUSH /TOOTHPASTE/ MOUTHWASH/ FLOSS/ COTTON BALLS /TISSUES
- NAIL CARE SUPPLIES/ HAND LOTIONS/ HAIRBRUSH

SCHOOL SUPPLIES:
- PLANNER/ ORGANIZER
- PENCIL SHARPENER
- PAPER CLIPS/ RUBBER BANDS /TACKS & PINS
- SCOTCH TAPE/ GLUE
- CALCULATOR
- STAPLER/ STAPLES/ HOLEPUNCH
- NOTEBOOKS/ FOLDERS
- PAPER/ PENS/ PENCILS
- HIGHLIGHTERS/ POST-ITS
- THUMB DRIVE(S)
- RULER/ SCISSORS

ELECTRONICS & HOUSEWARES:
- POWER STRIPS/ BATTERIES
- LAMP/ DESK LAMP
- TV/ DVD/ BLU RAY PLAYER
- STEREO/ IPOD / GAMING SYSTEM
- ALARM CLOCK
- COMPUTER/ PRINTER/ EXTRA PRINTER INK
- FAN
- SMALL COFFEE MAKER
- PRINTER plus USB CABLE

Pamela Ellis, The Education Doctor®, has helped thousands of teens attend a college that feels like home. She brings 25 years of experience in education to assist with college selection, admissions, financial aid, and freshman transition success. Dr. Pamela holds a PhD from Stanford and MBA from Dartmouth. For tips and tools to help your college-bound teen, visit compasscollegeadvisory.com.

Bonus: Tips and Resources for Parents of College Students

Books

- *Generation Z Goes to College* by Corey Seemiller and Meghan Grace
- *How to Raise an Adult* by Julie Lythcott-Haims
- Letting Go: A Parents' Guide to Understanding the College Years by Karen Levin Coburn and Madge Lawrence Treeger

Useful Websites

- collegeparent.org
- collegeparentcentral.com
- The parent page for your teen's college (if you can't find one, ask the freshman office where to find this resource)

Conclusion

Throughout this book, I have called for a redefined approach to college admissions that gives your teen ownership of the process yet the parent is still the parent. I recently spoke on a panel of educators in Chicago, and a parent in the audience asked the panel to express our views on the "problems" in education.

My response: "Parents are afraid to parent."

Parents today tend to be in one of two camps. Either they parent by absolving themselves of traditional parent responsibilities by being "friends" with their teen. These parents have a hard time saying "no" because they are afraid to "upset" their child or be seen as a "bad" person.

The second camp includes those parents who control their teens. When I have worked with these types of parents as clients, their teens resented their lack of freedom. One of my students lamented, "I wanted to set up my own SAT account so I could check my scores." Really? If the parent controls his/her teen, then it will be even more difficult for the teen to launch into adulthood. The "controlling" parent is afraid to just let go.

I've been afraid as a parent many times over. Afraid that I will make a wrong choice, afraid that I will forget a deadline, afraid that I will hold my teen back, afraid that my teen will resent me, afraid that my teen will think that I don't love him/her for who he/she is... There will always be something to fear in our role as a parent, and that role gets redefined with each stage of our teen's life.

My hope is that you will take from this book what you need to stop second-guessing yourself as you support your teen towards achieving his/her educational vision and reaching his/her best potential.

Glossary

ACT - American College Testing.

AP Courses - Advanced Placement Courses.

College Scholarship Service (CSS Profile) – an application to determine a family's eligibility for non-government financial aid; administered by College Board.

CommonApp (The CommonApp) – an application system that students may use to apply to any of the 700+ member colleges and universities.

Core Curriculum – program of study with specific courses that all students must take regardless of their majors, in order to meet graduation requirements.

Distributed Curriculum – a flexible program of study that requires students to take courses in particular areas of study to meet graduation requirements. For example, a college with a distributed curriculum may require that students take a natural sciences course. Within that category of natural sciences, there could be any number of courses from which students can choose.

Early Action (EA) – a non-binding college application policy that allows students to learn the admission decision, usually by January of senior year. Students offered admission have the same commitment deadline of May 1 as students admitted in the Regular Admissions decision process.

Early Decision (ED) – a legally binding college application policy that requires any student admitted to attend the college, regardless of any financial award.

EFC - Expected Family Contribution – a measure of your family's financial strength.

Free Application for Federal Student Aid (FAFSA) – an application to determine a family's eligibility for government financial aid; administered by US government.

FastApps - expedited e-mail invitations/applications used by some colleges for recruitment.

FSEOG - Federal Supplemental Educational Opportunity Grant – a federal grant awarded to students who have additional need beyond the Pell Grant.

Gap/Bridge Year Programs – special programs held between completing high school and beginning college; can be either a semester-long or full year program.

HBCU – Historically Black Colleges and Universities.

International Baccalaureate (IB) Program – a rigorous academic program that is internationally recognized as the gold standard in high school curriculum.

IEP - Individual Education Plan – a school-based plan that outlines any special learning issues, such as hearing impairment, development delay or emotional disorders, so that a student gets mandated instructional assistance.

ISEE - Independent School Entrance Examination.

Link to Pamela Ellis' email address - drpamela@theeducationdoctor.com.

Link to Pamela Ellis' website - theeducationdoctor.com

MBTI - Myers-Briggs Type Indicator is a questionnaire that can be useful for understanding how a student processes information, makes decisions, and relates to the outside world. The results can be used to help identify best-fit schools.

Open Curriculum – program that allows students to choose which classes they want to take.

PSAT - Preliminary Scholastic Aptitude Test – scores of test taken in October of junior year are used to qualify students for National Merit Scholarships.

Restricted Early Action (REA) – college application policy that restricts a student to applying to only one Early Action college deadline.

Regular Admissions – standard application policy for freshman admissions. All students admitted during Early Action and Regular Admissions cycles can notify the colleges of their decision by May 1 of senior year.

Rolling Admissions - This is an admission policy where the college considers each application as soon as all required information (such as high school records and test scores) has been received, rather than setting an application deadline and reviewing applications in a batch. Colleges that use a rolling admission policy usually notify applicants of admission decisions quickly.

SAT - Scholastic Aptitude Test.

SSAT - Secondary School Admission Test.

STEM - Science, Technology, Engineering, Mathematics

Tracking - a practice of grouping students of same age and ability to be taught together.

About the Author

Pamela Ellis, MBA, PhD—also known as The Education Doctor®—has helped hundreds of young people successfully navigate the college-admissions process.

Dr. Pamela graduated from Stanford University and the Tuck School of Business at Dartmouth College, and she earned a doctorate from the Stanford University School of Education. As CEO of Compass Education Strategies and a leader of operations at Compass College Advisory, her experience with the education system includes advising school districts, community organizations, and institutes of higher education.

As a result of her research into student transitions from high school to college—and evaluating the ways colleges successfully retain their student populations once admitted—she developed The Education Doctor® curriculum. She has visited more than 400 colleges and universities internationally to gain insight into their varying cultures and to explore the range of academic and social opportunities available to students on campus. Her research areas include high school to college transition, parent engagement, African-American males in academic pipeline, and college completion.

She lives in Dayton, Ohio with her family.

Made in USA - Kendallville, IN
1140055_9781976409325
07.22.2020 0813